Ancient Aliens

Ancient Aliens and Secret Societies

(Ancient Aliens the Unseen God and Modern Chronic Disease)

Debra Estrada

Published By **Simon Dough**

Debra Estrada

Ancient Aliens: Ancient Aliens and Secret Societies (Ancient Aliens the Unseen God and Modern Chronic Disease)

ISBN 978-1-77485-739-7

No part of this guidebook shall be reproduced in any form without permission in writing from the publisher except in the case of brief quotations embodied in critical articles or reviews.

Legal & Disclaimer

The information contained in this ebook is not designed to replace or take the place of any form of medicine or professional medical advice. The information in this ebook has been provided for educational & entertainment purposes only.

The information contained in this book has been compiled from sources deemed reliable, and it is accurate to the best of the Author's knowledge; however, the Author cannot guarantee its accuracy and validity and cannot be held liable for any errors or omissions. Changes are periodically made to this book. You must consult your doctor or get professional medical advice before using any of the suggested remedies, techniques, or information in this book.

Table Of Contents

Introduction

The subject of Ancient Aliens has recently exploded in popularization. In large part due to the numerous books and popular TV shows about the subject, many people are intrigued by whether we were visited by aliens in the distant time.

It appears from a contemporary perspective the recorded record of history come up relatively recently in the timeline of time. It is hard to locate precise writing from the past that dates past 3500 B.C. and it is a fact that there aren't any authentic historical documents written in any discernible language past the 5000th year B.C.

In such a short time in recorded time, one can only wonder whether the civilized human civilization was somehow helped by the sudden emergence of technology from alien beings. This theory definitely provides an enormous space for the imagination, curiosity and study.

In this book I've tried to cover a wide variety of topics and ideas that continue to arise when we consider the issue about ancient aliens. I hope that you find this information as stimulating, fascinating and fascinating like I did in my pursuit of an ancient alien world.

Chapter 1: Ancient Ufo Sightings

Since the beginning of time, humans have gazed with wonder in the sky at night. While humans sat and watched the captivating motions of stars across the black sky they realized that the shifting patterns of the stars exactly matched the seasons that change on Earth. This led them to design calendars and plan for the planting of crops.

However, some celestial objects didn't follow a consistent path, or any other pattern. They appeared to be averse to the designs of stars. Unidentified flying objects known as UFO's, created the human race with a new challenge and triggered a debate that persists until today.

Despite the recent popularity of the idea that UFOs might have visited the Earth in the past, a lot of people including the majority of scientists, remain extremely skeptical of the idea. Ancient peoples observed strange phenomena in the sky. They believed that they were gods because they believed their lives were governed by gods. In the majority of cases, it's easy to come up with multiple explanations. These ancient peoples might not have been aware of cosmic phenomena such as comets or meteors, it could be something else that were undiscovered by the primitive peoples however, these ancient societies interpreted these as supernatural events.

Although a significant portion of these events can be described, there are some that are elusive. One of the first recorded accounts of a meeting with an UFO is directly from Ancient Egypt. There's a tale of the Egyptian Pharaoh who observed flames across the skies. At first , he noticed one, but within a few days they were numerous across the sky. In fact, the Pharaoh was so impressed he kept the specific details of the incident written down on the papyrus. The translation's excerpts are the following:

"In The year 22 from the month that was the 3rd of Winter, at the sixth hour of the day, [...] in the Scribes in the House of Life it was discovered that a bizarre Fiery Disk was coming in the sky. ...

4

After a couple of days after which they increased in number on the sky, more than they had ever been. They glowed in the sky longer than the light of the sun. They reached the limit of the four support points of heaven. [...] The most powerful was the location in their Fiery Disks.

... It was ordered that the incident be recorded by His Majesty's records within The Annals of the House of Life to be preserved for ever."

The documents are of Pharaoh Tuthmosis 1480 B.C. [1]

The main hypothesis of historians for a long time have always been that man is the only one in the universe and that there are no aliens in space, no advanced civilizations other than our own , and that our civilization is among the most technologically advanced. If you believe in those beliefs, you will face a lot of difficulty in explaining many of these old stories, that are mysterious.

As we progress through history we are able to find more in-depth accounts of UFO's that go back to the present. There is a point where the consensus has been shifted to the point that most believe that there must be something to be behind every one of these UFO reports. They cannot be explained.

Chapter 2: Development Of Ancient Alien

Theory

The theory of Earth having been visited by aliens from the past is becoming more popular because of the numerous television shows and books that investigate this concept. This theory about the distant past of our planet would start with an alien spacecraft circling Earth and finding humans living in primitive and primitive existence. In awe and terror the primitive people could watch the as they fell of these fiery gods from heaven. Spacecrafts would have come down on Earth and committed strange acts and then departed. Today, the stories of their voyages are told by different cultures , each with their own distinct tales and legends.

The theory really gained popularization when the book 'Chariots of Gods' was published by Swiss creator Erich Von Daniken.

"I attempted to prove that the world was visited by aliens from space many times throughout the past. In addition, I believe that one of these initial visits is the reason the homo-sapiens became intelligent, therefore, they were able to mash up with our forefathers and triggered a sort of artificial mutation. Finally, these trips from space have gotten into every religion in mythology, as well as in some instances, they have been turned into archeological artifacts." -- Erich Von Daniken

It is well-known the fact that Daniken is the author of millions of titles around the world , and continues to be very popular despite the fact that some ideas have been challenged by research and opinions that are contrary to his.

The reason for his popularity is partly due to his constant challenge to generally accepted theories of history. While his theories are rejected by traditional scientists, they've certainly gained a following with the general population.

Daniken spends a great deal of time in the world in search of evidence to back his theories. People are fascinated by his discoveries and many are concerned that the conventional perspective on world history may be flawed in many ways.

What is it that makes Daniken's ideas so well-known? One person who researched Daniken's popularity and was an expert on the subject of extra-terrestrial intelligence was late Carl Sagan.

"We are intelligent beings, we are intrigued and enthralled by the way the world works. We seek out the extra-ordinary and if you think of these claims, if only they were true, they would be amazingly interesting; that we have been visited by beings from elsewhere who not only have created our civilization for us but mated with human beings...in my view much more likely to have mated with a Petunia than an extra-terrestrial...but certainly there is a degree of fascination if such accounts were true." - Carl Sagan

Von Daniken has had a solid skin to the kind of wry skepticism that he has exhibited.

"I recognize and acknowledge that this theory is not going to be accepted by conservative scientists, but it has always been the case There isn't a single simple theory that is proven to be true that has convinced the scientists. For instance, those first cave drawings that were found in Spain in caves, and elsewhere and the entire archaeological world was against it. they all thought"it's false, it's not true'. But it's not. It typically takes an entire generation, or even up to ten or twenty years before the new theory is accepted." Erich Von Daniken

The passage of time has proved Daniken in a way, as the foundations of his theories are just as well-known today like they've ever been.

The theories of Daniken may not have stood up to scrutiny, of course. The pyramids , for instance are a prime example. Daniken declared that they could not have been built without the assistance of extraterrestrial intelligence.

The pyramids' designs that we know today are believed to be the culmination of a long-running process of trial and failure. A hundred years before the construction began in Giza the Egyptians constructed structures along the shores of the Nile for use as tombs. These were underground chambers known as Mastabas constructed out of mud that had been dried in the sun. From these simple tombs emerged the pyramids of the real kind, but the first ones were in Saqqara and were step pyramids , such as the one that was built by King Joseph.

Pyramids of King Joseph was the first pyramid to be constructed with passages, tombs and tombs beneath. A smaller pyramid with a stepped design was constructed on top of it and a larger structure was added, leaving the one that remains today. It was to be the template for subsequent pyramids.

The structure of Joseph's pyramid is due to the structure of the walls with buttresses that tilt inwards towards the center.

However, the subsequent pyramid was not as effective. The Egyptians attempted to construct the pyramid with a higher elevation, but the outside was smashed into a pile of rubble. Through trial and trial and with the perfect angle found in the grand pyramid at Giza that we are all familiar. There are those who believe that they couldn't succeed without assistance from extraterrestrial intelligence. However, the idea is not a simple one to believe.

Even though certain of Daniken's theories are contested, one will deny that he has played a key role in promoting the concept of contact with aliens from the past. Through his constant and unwavering publicizing, he's contributed more to bringing ancient alien theories to the attention of a wider audience than any other in the history of science.

For a comprehensive overview on the opposing theories, readers are advised to watch the remarkable documentary made by Chris White, which disproves a number of the assertions made by some of the most popular theorists of ancient aliens.

Chapter 3: Ancient Artifacts

Artifacts that are discovered around the globe typically provide a silent account to the past of a civilization , and the way they attempted to comprehend celestial events. For instance, there is the great ceremonyal centre called Tiwanaku located in Bolivia. The site is also called Puma Punku.

It's not as ancient or striking as the ancient pyramids of Egypt What makes this location so special is its particular place of origin. There is a belief that it was not possible to have been constructed without the help of an advanced intelligence.

Like the blocks found at Giza The Tiwanaku area has huge stones at Tiwanaku with a weight of more than 100 tons, which were transported across 10 kilometers from quarry that was the source of the stones. The massive stones were used to construct massive structures that were at more than 12,000 feet above sea level in a region in which it is almost impossible to grow food. The elevation is so high that the plants emerge from the soil stunted. The Tiwanaku had a deep understanding of modern techniques for agriculture that allowed their crops to flourish and produce food in spite of their harsh environment.

The structure that appears in the picture below features a central figure that is carved into it by Viracocha the pre-Inca, an ancient god whom the people of Tiwanaku believed that came out of the ocean.

The Gate of the Sun located at Tiwanaku, Bolivia

It is said that this was achieved by massive laborers using ropes to transport these massive stones across land but it is unclear the existence of 'Nephilim' or giants in existence in that time and were able to assist in the movement of these stones from one spot to another. The Tiwanaku who flourished from around around 300 A.D. to 900 A.D. might have tried to reach out to aliens using their intricate creations and stunning structures. They perished in the year 1100 A.D. from extended drought.

***

There are also the Nazca lines that are located in Peru. With more than 200 square kilometers, an awe-inspiring design of massive artwork adorns on the Nazca plateau. Alongside photographs of spiders, birds and animals, long straight lines extend to every point of the compass. While it is true that these lines are a representation that reflect their cultural values, it's difficult to comprehend why anyone could create a picture so vast that it is able to only be observed in the sky.

The lines and images only seen from the air. at ground level , you can only observe the slight movement and alignment of stones that are on the ground.

A Nazca line that runs through the ground.

Nazca lines Nazca lines are believed to have been constructed around 400 A.D. to 650 A.D.

View from the air of Nazca Lines

The images could be created with the intention of communicating with aliens from the skies.

They are truly amazing surface artifacts created by moving small pebbles and rocks that creates a change in the hue of the that lies in desert. It is evident that the majority of these patterns are designed to be oriented towards heaven in some manner. The precise reason the reasons for these patterns is unclear, however one can suppose that it has something to do with their traditions and culture.

Maybe the Nazcans were projected by the Nazcans in the sky, and used the images for ceremonial and religious reasons. They could have been created by a few skilled artists belonging to Nazca society. Nazca society. The Nazca lines truly are an unsolved mystery because nobody is the certain purpose they were intended meant to serve. Much like the world's ancient history it is an unspoken record of the activities that have occurred in the past. Time has revealed the truth of the reason behind their origins.

There are many artifacts that have been discovered that seem to have been influenced by extra-terrestrials. For instance, here is an ancient piece of Mayan jewelry that appears to be an aircraft of some sort.

or this Mayan artifact, which resembles an astronaut:

Mayan Sculpture from Tikal, Guatemala

Some have even suggested that the plane is an image of a bird, fish or another animal, and that the astronaut is merely an elaborate mask for a ceremony of some kind. It's hard to find conclusive evidence since the ancient civilizations have produced a myriad of bizarre objects, many of that were simply reflections of their wisdom and habits. Some of their works are impressive in their size and the skills required to make these items. For instance:

Olmec Culture, Mexico

The massive stone was found in Mexico. The obsidian-carved sculptures were made in the hands of Teotihuacan people. They had more than 200,000 people in the period of 1000 B.C. and they were located 30 miles to the north from Mexico City. They constructed their famous Pyramid of the sun which featured a 720-foot base that was also 200 feet high. It was nearly identical to the massive Giza pyramid. Giza.

It is hard to locate solid evidence of ancient alien influences from artifacts, mainly because there are many false claims being made in this field. The crystal skull, the ancient written works mysterious treasures of every kind have been fabricated by evil people throughout the history of mankind. The process of separating fact from fiction requires time and careful , in-depth research.

A relic from the past which caught my eye when reading this book can be seen in the Metropolitan Museum of Art in New York City. The drum that is in this picture originates originated from Peru and is visible in the picture below:

2nd- 1st century B.C. - Peru[3]

The drum's ancient design depicts the humanoid form with a head that is exaggerated on the top. Particularly interesting is the design of the head that has protrusions that point towards the ears and nose with no neck and a slit to open the mouth.

The 'alien' character is in direct correspondence to one of the more intriguing instances of abduction by aliens of the present era - the Pascagoula incident. 4. Charlie Hickson gave a description of an alien being He met in 1973. It is an artist's rendition:

This is the type of similarity that may provide evidence of the presence of aliens in the past. Many of the technological capabilities of the ancient civilizations is difficult to put attributing to extraterrestrial influence however we can expect to observe instances where they used alien imagery in art, which is similar to our current experience. Some believe that the rapid growth of civilization in general could not have happened without intervention from extraterrestrials.

In spite of the general large theory, this specific instance of the 'no neck style of the aliens is a compelling possibility of depicting an alien being in the ancient society.

Chapter 4: Additional Historical And More

Ancient Information

In the ancient times of Egypt In the town of Abydos within the Temple of Seti I, an inscription was written using objects that resemble the shape of a spacecraft, a submarine and helicopter. What exactly these objects represent is to be determined. The hieroglyphs date back to 1294 B.C. up to 1279 B.C.

Hieroglyphs of Ancient Egypt

Close-up 1 - Helicopter

Close up 2 Submarine

Close-up 3 Spacecraft Spacecraft

Sometimes, we need to be cautious not to fool ourselves into not seeing what we would like to be seeing. The images above provide a great example. Let's take a look at the helicopter once more:

First of all, notice that the "propeller" touches the tail and no helicopter will be able to make it any distance even if the rotor gets into the tail. What happens is the case if we're actually viewing the side view of the tomb? In this next picture, an Egyptian coffin has been superimposed onto the original image

Perhaps the artist who designed the hieroglyphs was merely trying to depict the sarcophagus or coffin? It is possible to see the first image of a scarab as well as the third one as a fish, but because we are seeking out foreign images, our brain may fool us into thinking that we are seeing what we really would like to see.

Another illustration is the front cover of this book. The cover image is believed to be an ancient Egyptian offering an offer to some other however when illuminated and lit, the image appears to be just the tallest vase or receptacle that contains plants of some kind:

It is evident that when looking at the old alien issue it is important to be neutral to avoid seeing the things we want to or believe we will be able to see, and instead discern the truth of an event that could be hidden below the surface or even beyond the initial perception. It is normal to connect images with things that we are familiar with in our modern world. It's possible to conclude that there were no helicopters flying around during the times of the ancient Egypt Masons and craftsmen were likely creating images of objects which they were accustomed to their society at the moment in time.

If someone is able to prove that there are pictures of helicopters on the ancient Egyptian tombs, the story can have an inclination to be repeated time and time again particularly in the current "viral" age. What happens is that you have an alternate version of history or pseudo-history that is being constructed in the minds of the general public. It is a nice way of describing a piece of history that is completely incorrect. The issue is that in some cases, a particular version of history is based on opinion. We can take a look at historical facts and come to two different conclusions based on our bias, beliefs, and so and so on.

Chapter 5: Space Mysteries And Ufo Shapes

In the spring of 1972, pioneer 10 set off for a trip towards the stars. It carried an invitation to the inhabitants of Earth. The ship's hull is decorated with a plaque that informs us the story of who we are and where we are and our contact number for the heavens. Pioneer has quit the solar system and has traveled far beyond the reach of Earth. It is unknown if the message will ever be heard. It is traveling at a distance of 250,000 miles per hour from our sun, researchers inform us it is likely that Pioneer 10 will travel towards the directions of stars Aldebaran (A star located in the Constellation Taurus) and will eventually get there within two million years.

The image is from the Pioneer 10 Plaque

There could be several civilizations living among the stars, and getting in touch with them is among humanity's most exciting experiences. Have you made contact with them? Has it been established? Are there any chances that astronauts from other planets have already visited Earth and left their contact card here on Earth?

We should consider the limits of time when considering aliens. If you think about the fact it that Pioneer 10 will take 2 million years to reach a star which is very close to Earth in the scope of our galaxy; it begins to provide us with a view of the time limit. Even if a spacecraft were to be able to travel at the speed of light: more than six hundred million miles an hour (about 27,000 times more that Pioneer 10) the vast distances in the universe would cause space travel to be a slow process. It would take about twenty five thousand years to reach the nearest galaxy.

Of course , we can think about hyper-warp travel such as star wars, or traveling through "stargates," "portals, and wormholes. This kind of science fiction travel method would permit immediate travel from one region within the Universe to another , or possibly even travel to other universes.

However, let's take a break from the'star-trek'-type options for a second. Imagine that we're dealing with spacecrafts that must obey Physics laws with which we are accustomed. We can say that they are equipped with anti-gravity technology, which allows the aircraft to fly more quickly and maneuver more quickly than previously known aircraft for military use. But let's assume that they are still physical objects dependent on distance and time restrictions. Their inhabitants are organic living things with similar limitations.

What is the 2 most commonly used UFO shapes? Saucer-shaped and cigar-shaped. What do we know in our technology, which is saucer-shaped or cigar-shaped?

Cigar-shaped human device

Saucer-shaped human device

What is the reason these devices are shaped in this way? They are designed to withstand high pressure from deep sea. A few deep sea bathyscaphes are also circular in shape, like some UFO's.

If we launch spacecraft into space, they're generally not aerodynamic. Look at Apollo Lunar Lander or the International Space station; they are not required to stand up to high pressure or have an aerodynamically sleek profile. This is how Pioneer 10 looks like:

Pioneer 10

Because it's traveling through space, it doesn't require the excessive pressure. Why can't we find UFO's that look like this? Why aren't UFOs equipped with large antennae, awry landing gear that are exposed, struts exposed, and so and so on?

Could it be due to UFO's have to go underwater? Only a tiny portion of the oceans in the world have been explored. The form of UFO's could provide us with an insight into their origins and needs for travel. It could be possible that the majority of UFO's are not from outer space, but rather come from "inner space' beneath Earth.

This concept is more sensible than the necessity of traveling millions of miles across long periods of time. Scientists are uncovering new species of animals every day, so who's to say there aren't subterrestrials in the oceans beneath the planet Earth?

Chapter 6: Unidentified Submerged Objets

Earth has a total surface that is more than 195 million square miles , and nearly two-thirds of this area is covered in water. Even to this day the majority of the oceans and oceans have remained largely unexplored. We have more knowledge about the mysteries of the moon's surface than we know about the oceans that cover the globe.

As long as it has been documented eyewitness stories of UFOs appearing in the sky There have also been reports of similar UFO's unknown submerged objects, however these reports aren't so widely publicized.

A USO is essentially an UFO that can go in and out of water. In fact, you could describe UFOs and USO's as being one and the same It's just that a UFO transforms into an USO once it has submerged.

The 11th of October 1492 has been recorded as one of the earliest instances of an eye-witness account of the events of

USO. It was actually a occurrence on the Santa Maria which was one of the vessels of Christopher Columbus. At 10:10 pm on that day, it was a clear and calm night, and Christopher Columbus and his crew were traveling across one of the deepest parts in the Atlantic in the region that is which is now referred to by the name of Bermuda Triangle. Below them lay nearly the length of four miles (about 22,000 feet in depth).

Then, suddenly, lights appeared appearing beneath on the waters surface. A member of the team members noticed an object in the shape of a disc rising out of the water . It released a lighting flash that astonished Columbus and his 120-strong crew on board the three-ship fleet. They were five hours from their exploration of America.

The diary that Columbus kept on board his ship details what can be described as an UFO or USO incident. Columbus said it was 'the flickering of a candle moving upwards and downwards in the dark'. It couldn't have been the result of a campfire since they were not visible from the shore's horizon.

This incident could be more than just a legend. Original documents of Columbus' journal have been preserved by Fordham University and copies of the journal's handwritten entries are available for study and translation.

The 11th of October 1492 sighting wasn't an isolated incident. Over the course of two months, Columbus observed a myriad of odd events, including unproved sightings both in the sky and at sea.

***

One of the first European sightings was reported at the time of 1067, in England. There was a report of seeing a bizarre thing in the sky coming down to Earth shining brightly across the countryside. It came down and then rose again. After it returned down another time before it fell into the ocean. [5]

***

A much earlier glimpse of the USO's, which can be considered to be ancient, dates dating back to 329 B.C. in the year 329 B.C. Alexander the Great was said to have observed glowing shield-like objects flying in or out of Jaxartes River (now known as the Syr Darya River) in India. The sighting enthralled him to the point where the great Alexander put all his efforts into trying to locate them and some also believe that Alexander tried to discover the lost city of Atlantis.

***

It is believed that the Santa Catalina channel is a 26 mile long stretch that is part of the Pacific Ocean that separates the city of Los Angeles from Catalina Island. According to some, these waters some of which may extend as far like Mount Everest is high, could hold secrets that are mysterious submerged objects that are not identified.

Catalina Island itself has been the location of many UFO sightings. Recently, there were reports of unknown submerged objects flying in channels and flying out. There are estimates that there were hundreds of of UFO reports within the area surrounding the channel. Preston Dennett authored a book entitled, "UFO's over California The UFO's

Over California' and has been researching UFO activity in the area for several years.

"There was a massive wave of sightings in the Santa Monica Mountain Range on June 14 on the 14th of June, 1992. The witnesses counted around 200 objects. What's fascinating about this particular case is that these objects were seen from below. Normally, when someone is able to see a UFO, it appears out of the sky, like the shape of a star, and then it is seen swooping towards the ground. They came from below and the sky above." Preston Dennett Preston Dennett

June 14th on the 14th of June, 1992 at 10:24 pm. for more than two minutes, The waters in the Pacific Ocean exploded with light as hundreds of disc-shaped craft were seen emerging from the water together. Like other reports from the USO, these vessels were seen to emerge in total silence. They remained in the air for a while before each took off and flew into the air.

The incident was reported as having occurred and were reported to various police agencies in the area as as Malibu. Here is a real transcription of one of those calls:

The Deputy: Lost Hills Sheriff's Station

Contact: Does anyone have any strange events tonight?

Deputy The Deputy: Oh, ...can we be a bit more specific. Ohh ....strange you say...

Caller: Lights.

Deputy: Lights?

Caller: Yes.

Deputy: What did you experience on your return trip?

Caller: I'm embarrassed to admit it because I'm afraid that you'll think that I'm crazy. We observed what we believed was a bright light over the sky.

Deputy: Okay.

The caller said we could tell that it wasn't a helicopter. I'm saying to you, I've not been more scared in my entire life.

***

According to Dennett the incident was signaled to U.S. Coast Guard in Long Beach which ultimately declined to conduct a thorough investigation. The incident in 1992 was the second incident in Los Angeles in three years.

In the morning fog on February 7 1989, divers as well as boat sonar systems and people who were on the shore observed an extended dark, unidentified craft diving out of the Pacific. For nearly ninety seconds, the USO lay just beneath the surface before it released about twelve smaller, fast-moving objects. Sixty seconds after that, the craft sank back to the bottom. The last time it was reported that sonar's direction was to the south, towards Santa Catalina Channel. Santa Catalina Channel before it went under the water and disappeared.

" ...and it was a plethora of objects which were observed in the waters off Marina Del Ray. Sometimes, these smaller boats, ranging from 20 feet to twenty feet in size, were observed under the ocean's surface and then they would move out and in the ocean." Preston Dennett Preston Dennett

The 1947 incident at Roswell brought about a global fascination with flying saucers, the incidents near Los Angeles also sparked a study of the capabilities and risks of the so-called USO's.

The oceans of the globe comprise 70percent of our globe and conceal a wealth of mystery. There is a possibility that oceans may be the home of sentient creatures since no one goes to them. It's fascinating to think of "underwater UFO's" since it is possible they have more knowledge about the world than we do.

One of the most striking aspects of the USO's tend to multiply and then break up. One of these cases is now known as"the Gulf of Nuevo event. In the time of the Gulf of Nuevo, the Argentinean Navy was on high alert in the search for two submarine-like underwater objects within its territorial waters. They believed they were American submarines.

In the end, as per reports, underwater objects can be seen in sonars to break up and then fall out of the water.

Two massive objects were discovered in the year 1960. They then miraculously expanded into six more objects. The Argentineans could not find them since they disappear. This story even attracted notice by the Soviet Union at the time. Nikita Khrushchev who was the head in the Soviet Union at that time was so enthralled by the entire tale that he was able to send his diplomatic attache to Buenos Aries to find out the details of what was going on.

Some researchers believe that these incidents may be just military submarines firing torpedoes others contend that submarines were incapable in firing 6 torpedoes all at once in 1960.

In the late UFO researcher Ivan T. Sanderson wrote an article in 1970 entitled "Invisible Residents'. He was credited as one of the first researchers to examine this USO phenomenon.

In his book, he wrote an additional remarkable instance of USO conduct. In the month of March, 1963 an U.S. Navy Submarine exercise was going as planned

100 miles from in the waters from Puerto Rico. One navy submarine suddenly left its assigned route following the discovery of an unidentified craft moving at more than 150 knots. The crew members of the submarine are amazed by the depth to which the craft that is not identified is traveling... at 20,000 feet beneath the ocean surface.

The craft was emitting the sound signature of one propeller type of vehicle. A typical submarine would likely be crushed when it traveled further than 7000 feet. So this one did not outperformed the capabilities of every submarine in the day, and in fact nearly all submarines of today.

The object was followed for nearly an entire day by crew members of U.S. Navy subs and this craft was capable of speeding along at will, at nearly impossible speeds, and then stoppIng and rest for a while until the Navy was able to catch up with it.

The details of the event were relayed the Naval Headquarters in Norfolk Virginia However, an official determination regarding what was observed through sonar that day was not established. According to some accounts that there was a possibility that the Navy was lost in its vessel at midnight on the fourth day of discovery, and was not seen again by sonar.

There is no way to come up with a specific hypothesis about what could happen to something at that speed. There have been reports of UFO's floating in and out of the ocean however there is a lack of information about what was observed in 1963 off in the waters in Puerto Rico. UFO's, on the other hand are often observed, whereas USO's are mostly secret. If the Navy has more information regarding the location of USO's and UFO's, it's unlikely they would divulge the details to the public at large. In the past, it has been the U.S. Navy has attempted to deny UFO's as simply weather balloons.

Despite denials and denials, reports from all over globe continue to be reported. A different, astonishing incident was published in the world media on the 11th of November in 1972. A submarine-like object that was fast moving was discovered on sonar in Sonja Fiord off the west coast of Norway by the Norwegian Navy who hunted it over a period of two weeks. The Norwegian Navy had a fleet of surface vessels along with a few specially equipped helicopters for sub-hunters were employed to hunt for the object.

On the 20th November 1972, the USO is visible in the very first instance. The description of the USO was a huge silent cigar-shaped thing. The Norwegian Navy ship's fired at the craft but it quickly backed away from the assault. The navy then continued to launch depth charges but without results.

After about two weeks Navy officials decided that they would block the river in hopes of capturing the USO. They wanted to close off the fiord, so that no one could enter or exit. But in the span of 14-15 days, the USO disappeared , prompting many to believe it was not an ordinary submarine.

It is believed that USO's have the capability of traveling beneath the crust of Earth into layers that have not been discovered by humans. It was only recently revealed that scientists have found evidence of a huge reservoir of water that is three times larger than the oceans on Earth that are that lies hundreds of miles beneath the surface of our planet. [6]

If the results of these research prove to be true this would suggest that there is an undiscovered universe beneath earth's surface. Earth. The concept is repeatedly mentioned throughout the Bible. For instance, in Revelation chapter 5, verse 5

"And there was no one either in heaven, or on earth, nor under earth, could open the book, nor to read it."

Some might argue"under" the Earth refers to things that are in the ocean, but the following passage in Revelation 5 makes clear distinction between what is under the Earth and things that are located in the ocean.

"...every creature that is in heaven, as well as on earth, under the earth, as well as those that are found in the sea and all of the things that are within them ..."

The expanded version of the bible describes the underworld of the Earth as the 'place of the souls who have died as well as Hades.

Philippians Chapter 2 Verse 10 states the existence of beings beneath the Earth. Because we are considering some of the references in the Bible which leads us to the next chapter's topic.

Chapter 7: The Bible Record Of Aliens

For centuries, scientists have been wrestling with the question of what UFO's might be, as well as the possible identities of their occupants and where they might originate from. The earliest reports of UFO's can be found in those pages in the Bible. Even though it contains some minor errors in the context that are usually due to translation or transcription errorsthe Bible has incredible accuracy in relation to both prophetic and historical events.

In recent times In recent times, the Bible is increasingly being used by researchers as a source of stories that describe encounters with aliens as well as UFOs. Naturally, such a view is not without controversy. Is the traditional interpretation of biblical texts be called into question?

With the decreasing importance of religion for the majority of modern scientists, people are seeking alternatives which are more scientific. Instead of believing in the creation by God there are many who want to prove that the creation process was carried out by alien civilizations that are from the past. There's a strong need to know what God is, but people are looking for alternative explanations to satisfy their need for a meaningful but tasty the past.

The search for the first contact with alien beings prior to prehistoric times led to this particular scriptural location and the Bible's very first chapter, The book Genesis.

Genesis describes the conditions of this world prior to the earliest stages of the age of

"And it happened that the people began multiplying across the planet and daughters were also born to them.

The children of God observed their daughters and believed that they were fair, and they were able to get them wives from every woman they could choose...

There were giants on the earth during those times Also after that when the sons of God entered into the women of the world, and they bore children to them, they became powerful men who were in the past and men of fame."

Genesis chapter 6 verse 4

Who were these 'giants on the Earth and the'sons of God mention in the Bible text? Although most English Bibles employ the term "giants," the original Hebrew word is 'Nephilim'.. A translation of Nephilim is'men who fell or "those were who fell' meaning people who came down from the heavens. This doesn't necessarily mean that they were physically massive It could be that they were heroes who fell from the sky and created an hybrid race.

For many researchers who want to unravel the mysteries of UFO's from the past world It is believed that the Bible has other clues that are intriguing. Actually, depending on the reading, it's possible to say the Bible is filled with UFO references. One example is the account of Moses. 3500 years ago , the Bible tells of the story of how Israelites were released from slavery in Egypt. Under the direction of Moses they began the journey of forty years through the desert on the route toward the promised land. According to the Bible an uncanny thing guides the masses through the desert barren:

The Lord came before them during the dawn in the form of a pillar made of cloud, to guide them along through the path; and then at night, in a fire pillar to provide them with illumination; to travel through the day and at night.

He did not remove the cloud pillar during the day, nor did he remove the fire pillar at night, from the people. - Exodus chapter 13 verses 21-22

Many believe that the biblical passage has a different meaning that is long-cherished in the minds of Christians and Jews Some people believe that the pillar that is cloud-like and also the one of flame could be like an UFO that is shaped like a cigar and carries the Idea of extra-terrestrial intelligence, or an advanced intelligence, which is leading humanity.

Many of the most fascinating biblical texts concern Mount Sinai and the handing down of the Ten Commandments.

Then mount Sinai was all cloud of smoke, as the Lord came down on it with fire The smoke of it rose as the smoke from a furnace. The whole mountain was shook.

When the sound of the trumpet was long and ever louder, Moses spake, and God replied to him with the sound of a voice. - Exodus chapter 19 verses 18-19

After Moses came back with his Ten Commandments after his encounter with God at Mount Sinai, his skin mysteriously glowed with an unnatural glow. His hair was become to white as snow. The story of Moses is often attributed with an extraterrestrial event and some believe that his hair might be white because of radiation exposure. The notion that Israelites might have been guided towards the Promised Land by a sort of extraterrestrial force has drawn many believers over the past decade, however evidently, religious leaders and scientists are determined to oppose this theory.

This issue is primarily with interpretations and the issue of being controversial, because if you claim the idea that Jehovah is an extraterrestrial it would alter the foundations theology of Judaism or Christianity in a fundamental way.

However, it's a matter of interpretation. These are facts that are simple to speculate on. You can go through every single story in the Bible and see items that can be seen as evidence of an extra-terrestrial. But if you're going to be able to provide such an amazing explanation, you need to be able to prove it with evidence otherwise, these claims are viewed as just fantasies and just imagining.

Biblical connections to aliens as well as UFO's do not only exist in that book called Exodus. in the book 2 of Kings there is an interesting story of the prophet Elijah who lived 9000 years prior to the period of Jesus. As Elijah traverses the Jordan river together with Elisha an air-borne craft appears:

Then it happened that they continued to go along, and chatting when, behold it appeared a chariot of fire, as well as horses of fire, and they split the two in pieces And Elijah took off in an eerily fast whirlwind to heaven. Then Elisha was able to see it, and he shouted, My father my father the Chariot of Israel and the horsemen of it. He did not see him further... 2 Kings Chapter 2 verses 11 & 12. 2 Kings Chapter 2 verses 11 and 12

Many ancient civilizations have written about flying chariots which fly through the air. A lot of people believe that they are actually descriptions of UFOs.

A little more than three millennia after the ascend of Elijah to heaven on a chariot filled with fire, another astonishment happens. It's this time about the Hebrew prophet Ezekial. There are those who believe that he to have encountered spaceships from another dimension on at least four distinct occasions. In one of his accounts the author describes a clearly mechanical device that was under the control of human-like creatures.

When I looked around at the four wheels carved by cherubims. One wheel is by a cherub and another by a different Cherub. The look of these wheels were the hue of beryl stones.

As for their appearances, they shared a similarity to a wheel, as if it was in the middle of the wheel.

When the cherubims left through the air, the wheels passed by them. And when the cherubims raised up their wings and climbed up on the ground, the wheels did not turn behind them.

As they stood, they did not move; as they lifted they lifted themselves too: because their spirit was living within the midst of them.

The beauty of the Lord was removed from the doorway of the dwelling, and he walked over the Cherubims.

And the cherubims swung up their wings, and then swung above the earth before my eyes and when they left they saw the wheels right beside them.

- Ezekial chapter 10 verses 9,10,16 19

Based on this Biblical description of a mysterious flying device In the 1960's NASA Engineer Joseph Blumridge constructed a model like the one shown below:

Could this be the same as the vision that Ezekial was seeing? This could mean that Ezekial was having a vision inside his own mind , or the dream was just a dream. Perhaps he noticed something that he was unable to explain and therefore he described the vision as accurately as possible.

***

There is an amazing story in the Bible in which Peter receives instructions on how to reach out to the unbelievers. Peter is praying in the backyard of a home as we discover:

And (Peter) noticed that heaven was opened and a specific vessel falling upon him like it was an enormous sheet of cloth that was knitted at the four corners and let down to earth: Acts 10 verse 11.

Heaven was opened, and a vessel was descending!

If we study the passage in Acts 10, Verse 11, which is its first Greek version, the text is translated to: "and he beholds the heaven opened and descends on him a vessel with the size of a sheet and bound at four corners with four corners and laid down on the Earth"

In verse 16 we are told:

The process was repeated three times and the vessel raised again to heaven.

In verse 16, it does not mention 'the sheet was re-sealed the sheet was taken back up', but rather "the vessel".

A lot of people have read this text and then believe that Peter saw an unveiled sheet falling from the sky brimming with animals, but on close examination, it says that a vessel was lowered out of the heavens.

A representation of the vessel' Peter saw.

The above picture may be more like the one Peter observed and the creatures were inside the "dome" part. Most traditional paintings depict the sheet of linen that is holding creatures. It could be because the artist called it the sheet as he saw there were four edges tied like a sheet could be secured to a bed or mattress frame.

A few verses prior, Cornelius was visited by an Angel who advised Cornelius to meet

Peter and this Angel informed him of the exact location Peter is staying and as well as his full name, and that Peter had specific information for Peter.

It appears that based on the following Biblical text that evidence is available that certain alien vessels are connected to angels.

Many Christians are inclined to believe that aliens are demons or demons of the genesis. Actually, the Bible states that demons have a limiting ability when it comes to their capability to communicate with physical objects and manipulate them while angels are not subject to such a limitations.

Chapter 8: Angels Or Aliens

To go beyond the issue of aliens and angels, it is important to first comprehend the differences between them.

According to the Bible angels are divine beings who were designed by God. They are the servants of God and are able to take on both spiritual and physical form. Psalm 104 says that God gives his angels "spirits'. It also states that angels are able to disguise themselves as human beings without our knowledge, as mentioned in Hebrews chapter 13, verse 2:

Don't forget to entertain strangers; for this is how some have entertained angels without realizing.

It is crucial to recognize that angels aren't leprechauns or fairies; angels can't dance on top of a pin. They are like us. They could appear to be any human you may encounter on the streets.

In the Bible that Satan has angels. We can infer that Lucifer turned from God as well as gathered a host of angels along with him.

probably voluntarily joining the forces of Lucifer.

Matthew 25 , verse 41 is:

Then he will say to them on the left hand, Leave from me, you cursed, into the eternal fire that is prepared for Satan and his angels...

Isaiah Chapter 14 Verse 12-17 provides information about Lucifer who is a different name given to the devil. It also explains that he was also an angel himself:

How hast thou fallen from the heavens, Lucifer, the son of the dawn! How is thou mangled to the earth, and caused the nations to be weak!

You have said in your heart that I will ascend to heaven, and I will elevate my throne over all the stars that are in God I will be in the mount of the congregation, on the northern sides:

I will be ascended over the heights of the clouds. I will rise as high as the highest.

But thou will be dragged down to hell, down the bottom of the pit.

People who look at thee will be able to look at you with a narrow eye and think about thee, saying, "Is this the man who caused the earth to shake, and that shook kingdoms?

The world was made an unforgiving wilderness and destroyed the cities of it That did not let in the prisoner's house?"

It is interesting to observe the fact that Lucifer a.k.a. the devil will be observed by the public as a man. They are asked, "Is this the man?"

The hell we think of, the hell that we think of when we think of eternal fire was created by Satan and his angels and not for humans. Lucifer is an angel who, for some reason, refused to obey God which was accompanied by a variety of angels.

We hear of an armed conflict that was fought in heaven or is scheduled to take its place on the earth in the near future and is mentioned in Revelation chapter 12 verses 7-9:

There was conflict in heaven: Michael along with his angels battled against the dragon. The dragon fought, and Michael's angels,

The battle was not won nor was their place to be found in heaven.

And the dragon of great size was exiled and the serpent of old, known as the Devil and Satan that deceives the entire world: he was thrown out to the earth and his angels were thrown out along with him.

The angels as well as the devil are taken out of heaven. We also have to read the following passage in Luke chapter 10, verses 16-18:

The seventy-seven returned in joy, saying: Lord, even devils are submissive to us in your name.

And he told them, I saw Satan as lightning struck from the sky.

We can see that the angels and the devil are thrown out of heaven. In Jesus his time on Earth There was a lot of people affected by the "devils". As an example, the text of Matthew chapter 8 as well as Verse 16:

As the time came and they brought him those who were demon-possessed: and he shook off spirits through his word and healed all who suffered from illness...

These demons have been thrown out of heaven and can no are able to access their physical body. They are able to inhabit the human body or another living thing through gaining access to the insides of their bodies. For instance, Matthew 8 verses 30 to 32: Matthew 8, verses 30, and 32:

There was also a great escape from them, a group of swine that were eating.

The devils made a plea to him by saying: If you were to cast us out and we are thrown out, let us go to the swine herd.

He said to them"Go. And when they got out, they entered the swine herd And, look the entire herd of the swine raced swiftly down a sloping hill to the sea and drowned in the sea.

We now know that aliens are not devils since devils are spirits. We find this chapter 1 of Jude the first chapter verses 5-7:

And the angels who remained their former home and left their residence, God has placed in everlasting chains of darkness to the day of the day to come.

We can see that the bodily bodies of the angels who revolted and joined with Lucifer are being held in prison. We can conclude that Jesus probably bound the angels during his time unconscious for three days because Jesus had the chance to take on them, as was mentioned in Ephesians chapter 4 verses 8 and 9:

So he says, when the king ascended to heaven and led captives to their deaths, he commanded captivity and presented gifts to people.

(Now that he has ascended, what else is there to say other than that he descended as well into the lower regions on earth?

The physical angels who rebelled are known as devils and they are imprisoned below the Earth somewhere. The spirits of devils can wander the Earth and block living creatures , but because their bodies are imprisoned and cannot show up like angels are able to.

We look over the details in order that we understand that fallen angels, which is devils, are not exactly the same as aliens that have been witnessed piloting UFOs.

Moving to the 'good' angels. These are angels who serve humanity and follow the plans and instructions of God. They could fly UFO's in the event that they want to, because they possess bodies that are similar to human beings. They are so alike in reality, that if you happen to look at an angel it is possible to think they were human.

A few people get confused and think that angels must be twelve feet tall , with wings. They confuse angels and the cherubim. Cherubim are a particular kind of angel that has wings. Also, there are Seraphim who are also an angel type with six wings, but they have three wings. [8]

Returning to the good angels We've seen before that a vessel came from the heavens and appeared to Peter. Although no angels were visible in the boat, we're told that an angel appeared to talk to Cornelius who was aware of what was happening to Peter.

It seems that angels are able to access technology they can utilize to fulfill specific needs when needed. The craft could come up from the bottom of the Earth or beneath the oceans, and this is the cause of some of the UFO sightings seen throughout history.

Also it is likely that UFOs are not aliens from space, but are actually aliens within Earth. These aliens take off from beneath the oceans and then glide through the air; they are present through time, but haven't been identified. Angels are a form of advanced beings developed prior to the birth of humans , therefore they may possess advanced technology available to them.

One might ask why angels would fly spacecraft? If they are able of transforming into spiritual creatures and disappear at will[9], they certainly wouldn't have the need to fly a mechanical machine. Therefore, it's possible to conclude that we are likely to eliminate any angels as the people who pilot UFO's.

Chapter 9: Aliens In The Renaissance

We've seen in Chapter 5 how some of the earliest artifacts can be subject to an uninformed interpretation when interpreting them as evidence of aliens visiting Earth. The further back we go the more likely the evidence that we come across could be seen as cultural expressions from the local area or as random creative works.

Many ancient cultures had dragons or snakes in their artifacts and artwork. Theorists of ancient aliens believe that they represent extraterrestrials who visited the Earth in the past. Why do they believe this? In the first place, we need to be aware of the fact that ancient civilizations were affected through fallen angels. They were in the camp of Lucifer who was called serpent, snake or dragon. It is evident that the fallen angels attempted to persuade ancient cultures to join in a pledge of loyalty to Satan.

Keep in mind that this was prior to the time when all fallen angels were taken captive and imprisoned beneath the Earth which is the reason early cultures were greatly affected by these serpent and dragon images.

In reality, ancient alien theorists are right in their belief that the ancient civilizations were visited by extraterrestrials However, they are actually angels who have fallen. The ancient alien theorists aren't able to comprehend this because they remain under the influence of fallen angel spirits that continue to roam the Earth even though they don't be able to access their bodies. they can influence the thoughts of humans in the realm of spirit.

Then, in Revelation chapter 12, we are told:

The dragon of the deep was exiled the old serpent also known as the Devil and Satan that deceives all the world. He was thrown into the earth and his angels went out along with him.

There are four names here as dragon, serpent devil, dragon, and Satan. In addition, notice that his angels accompany his angels.

Then we read Isaiah chapter 27, verse 1:

In that time, the Lord with his ferocious and powerful sword shall slay leviathan the piercing serpent, or leviathan, the crooked serpent and he will kill the dragon in the sea.

We also have a title for the Devil. It is Leviathan and his place of residence as the sea.

We'll now turn our attention to the time of the Renaissance however, which is the time period from approximately 1350 A.D. to about 1650 A.D. In the Renaissance which is an French word that means "rebirth" or "re-birth" was an important time in the history of mankind when people allowed their souls, as well as their own were affected by angels. This is the time that we have a lot of vivid images of UFO's, for instance:

The image comes from it's from Palazzo Vecchio in Florence Italy. The painting is assigned to Jacopo del Sellaio, or Sebastiano Mainardi. The top right hand corner of the painting, there is an image of a shepherd looking upwards towards the heavens. Here are a few close-up pictures:

In this photo, the shepherd staring towards what appears be UFO.

Close-up of UFO or Nativity Star

A few researchers have attempted to prove that the painter was simply trying to depict the glory of God or the "Nativity Star". In a sense, they're right, but there is no doubt that the artist was painting the image of a UFO with an alien origin that we will explore in greater depth in the next chapter. Researchers are constantly coming up with new ways to discredit religious depictions of UFOs, as they're biased towards all things biblical. If the identical images were found in cave paintings of primitive civilizations , these experts would have been overflowing in awe of such evidence.

Here's another picture from a fresco dating around 1350:

Here are close-ups of images from right-hand and right corners:

Again, you can see that the artist has depicted UFO's in the night sky with people inside. This isn't some obscure cave painting nor any Mayan creature that has a tongue protruding. it is a straightforward image of the celestial landscape of some kind.

Another example, this painting dates from 1486, and is believed to belong to Carlo Crivelli. The painting's title is "The Annunciation of Saint Emidius The Annunciation with Saint Emidius'

Here's a closer view of the UFO shape disk that is emitting a beam light toward Mary:

It is evident in the details on the drawing that the painter has shown angels that are concentrically grouped around the heavens with a beam or a beam of God. It is evident that this artist was trying to depict an event that came from heaven in a spiritual manner.

There are a lot of other pictures from the Renaissance that show UFO's which appear to be. This is not surprising considering that the Renaissance was a period when humans were influenced by angels who visited their spirits in spirit form, as well as in spacecraft. The angels were able to affect their thinking and impart information that led to the rapid development of mankind.

Language, math high-end arts and music diverse science studies; all of these areas flourished at this period in the history of mankind and you could say that the amount of genius that arose at the time has not been replicated at such a large scale.

Chapter 10: The Star Of Bethlehem

In the previous chapter, we spoke about the "nativity star', also known as the UFO depicted in the painting of the Palazzo Vecchio in Florence Italy. Here's the image again:

We will now look at a different painting titled "The Baptism of Christ" that was created during 1710, by Flemish artist Aert De Gelder.

In this painting we observe that the artist has created a disc in the sky which is shining beams of light. This is a fantastic depiction on what the stars of Bethlehem might be like, and now you'll understand the reason. While this piece of artwork was intended to depict Christ's baptism Jesus but it could also make a great representation of the 'nativity'scene, the traditional scene of where Jesus became a baby.

Let me begin by saying that I've watched a variety of documentaries that have tried to find an explanation of what the protagonist of Bethlehem could be. One of them was made created by the History Channel, an American Cable Channel controlled by Walt Disney, the other was produced by Rick Larsen, a lawyer and independent researcher.

The majority of these studies assert they believe that the star that appeared in Bethlehem is an alignment between stars and/or planets at that specific time in the history of the world. They estimate the time of these planetary alignments around the year 1 B.C., the time of the demise of King Herod. The studies in general are complete and well documented with Larsen's results in particular are compelling. In spite of their well-thought-out ideas they do not reveal a crucial aspect of The Star of Bethlehem.

Let's examine Matthew chapters 2 and verses 1-13:

Then, when Jesus was born at Bethlehem of Judaea during the time of Herod the king, look out there were wise people from the east to Jerusalem,

And he asks"Where is he that was born as the King of Jews? We have seen his star rising in the east and have coming to worship him.

After Herod the king was informed of these words, he was worried, and everyone else in Jerusalem was with him.

When he had brought everyone of the chief priests, scribes and principals in one place, he asked them the place where Christ would be born.

They said to him:"In Bethlehem of Judaea For this is how it is written by the prophet

And and Bethlehem is in the country of Juda is not the least prince of Juda because from Bethlehem will arise an Governor, who will govern my nation of Israel.

Then Herod after he'd graciously called to the wise ones, enquired of them diligently at what time the star appeared.

He sent them to Bethlehem He said to them"Go and search for the infant When you find him, give me word, so to allow me to come and praise him as well.

After hearing the king's words, they left and then, behold, the star that they had seen at the eastern horizon, walked in front of them, and arrived and stood in front of the child's spot.

The moment they saw it, the were elated with great joy.

When they came to the dwelling they saw the tiny child along with Mary his mother. They were able to fall down and worship him. Then, after they had unveiled their treasures, they gave to him gifts: gold, frankincense, as well as myrrh.

Then, after being warned by God in a dream , that they would not be returning to Herod and departed for their own country in another manner.

When they had left from the place the angel of the Lord appears at Joseph through a vision telling him to get up, take the child and his mother and run to Egypt and stay there until I give thee word, because Herod is looking for the little child and destroy him.

In bold, I've highlighted two important phrases from the above bible passage. The first one is "the star that they observed in the east, was ahead of them until it came , and stood above the place where the little child was."

It should be evident that a combination between Jupiter and Venus is not able to be atop a spot that is on Earth. Actually, based on inference from the verse 11, it was above the house in which Jesus was.

A person on Earth could be led by a bright star such as the North Star sailors might follow a particular direction on the compass, such as North or East or West or South. The Magi may have followed a particular star or a combination of planets or stars to reach Jerusalem. Once they arrived in Jerusalem however, they were unable to find any further clues as to what direction to follow through the stars. If they did, then why should they stop to ask for directions?

Herod advised the people the to travel to Bethlehem just a few miles from Jerusalem and they then were again able to see the star, but this time, the "star" did not direct them in a straight line It was lowered and stood on the specific location.

Take a look at stars in the sky to convince me that it will lead someone to an exact house. It is not likely to take place. In the event that Jupiter as well as Venus or any other star fell on Earth in a way, it would wipe off the Earth which is an absurd explanation. If you attempt to find to follow a particular stars in the night sky might be able to travel in an extremely general direction, but it's impossible to identify a specific place on the Earth It's not rocket science, it's just logic.

When when the Magi left Jerusalem they observed a "star" which could guide them, as if hovering above the treetops in the distant. It was simply an UFO. Matthew considered it an amazing thing to see the same star that they had seen in the East and he's stunned as he recounts the events. The Magi are thrilled at the sight of the star. However, it is apparent that they had lost sight of the star that brought their journey to Jerusalem and this is a different'star" - a "star" that can fly above the earth so which a person can walk on the exact route, on the same street, and ultimately to a specific home which is a UFO, if there ever was one.

A second time, the angels appear before Joseph during a vision after the Magi depart. It was evidently the angel who was piloting the UFO that accompanied Magi. Magi to Jerusalem towards Bethlehem. The initial star that led those from West (probably Babylon) to Jerusalem could very well have been the result of the confluence of the planets and stars, according to the popular documentaries discussed earlier. It is apparent that the historical places of the stars match perfectly with dates and times at the date that Jesus was born. Jesus However, the second "star" mentioned within Matthew Chapter 2 Verse 9 can't possibly have been able be above a particular house area, allowing Magi to locate the infant Jesus living in a house in the presence of his parents.

Despite this shockingly evident conclusion one asks the majority of people who are Christian faith they'll say that the star appeared and landed above the spot where

Jesus was. They'd rather hold on to their unfounded belief rather instead of having to accept what could have happened.

I'm not trying to claim that all UFOs are controlled or piloted by angels, but this is only one of many instances in the history of mankind. There are probably many kinds of UFOs and as we gain more knowledge the universe, we'll surely discover a myriad of extraterrestrials and how they relate to the larger scheme of the universe.

Chapter 11: Grey Aliens

Our current topic on ancient aliens has led us through ancient artifacts, underwater UFO to demons and angels But what is the classic alien creature that we're familiar? The prototypical 'grey alien'.

This is the kind of aliens who were believed to have been discovered at Roswell and are also believed to be behind the notorious abductions of Betty as well as Barney Hill. 10. Is there evidence of aliens in grey that came from the time?

Here are some pictures that have been described by The Predionica Mask from prehistoric times located in the area of present day Kosovo.

It is believed that this mask is located located in The Kosovo Metohija Regional Museum and is believed to be associated with the old Ninca culture. One scholar[11] suggested that the mask could have been the source of inspiration for Ted Jacob's who designed the cover of Whitley Striber's highly acclaimed novel, Communion.

The cover of the book "Communion"

What do you think if Ted Jacob's not seen this artifact from the past? If that's the case, this is yet another fantastic illustration of an alien being in the past of society.

If we examine the typical almond-shaped eyes of the grey alien, we might speculate that they are required because of the lack the amount of sunlight in their usual environment. If the aliens lived below the surface of Earth and were living under the Earth, it would make sense that they would require larger eyes. Here's a screen-capture of a grey alien in an anonymous video uploaded to the internet in the year 2011.

Grey Alien

You can view a copy of this video along with commentary by clicking here:

http://youtu.be/A4dVcnik94M

This video features commentary from a person who is well-versed in CGI (computer generated images) as well as animatronics. He makes a convincing case for the authenticity that the film. In the event that you are not able to view the video, I've included the transcription below:

"I chose to write an analysis of this specific video here. Here, I'd like you to look at this incredible footage. As a professional watching this kind of footage over the past twenty years, I've not seen footage of aliens that I considered to be real, or even believed to be real. This footage is real. Look at how the eyes blink as well as examine this in-depth footage. The facial structure as well as the movementof the eye, it doesn't stretch like skin, but it is also able to move in a fluid motion, which isn't possible in CGI. What you need to know is one of the best ways to replicate the kind of motion that is fluid that you can replicate in CGI is to use a method that puts you've probably seen an image of a person wearing a black suit, with dots on the knuckles, and the like. It is necessary to put the dots on the eyes of something like this follow the movements otherwise it's basically motion-like because you'd have created the motion.

It's completely, every piece of it is fluid motion, which indicates that what we're seeing is real footage. It's true that I can say that what we're looking at isn't CGI. If you look across your forehead there's a lot of three-dimensional characteristics in the actual footage of an actual three-dimensional mean a person. There's no doubt about what we're seeing here.

On top of that thinking that this is some sort of amazing suit or anatomic doll is truly amazing. We have hands that look like this the ones in this video; take a look, they move. I'm talking about see at how long the thumb is. Also, this is footage. You can feel the wall's texture behind. You can also see how three-dimensional it is. It's all about looking at the shadows. Check out the shadowing. I'm talking about another thing. Every single shadow and line as well as lighting is perfect.

I've never witnessed CGI until today that doesn't require hiding the camera. I'm sure you are aware of what I am talking about. Take a look at the most recent fake video of aliens posted on YouTube and you'll notice that the time they employ CGI to make an alien appear it's only turning the camera on for a few seconds to ensure that you don't have time to take a seat and study the footage. Here we can see the full view. There is no attempt to conceal or cover everything.

The only thing I have found to disguise something can be the white and black. It appears to be a computer program. it appears that they removed the color and turned it into the black-and-white. Perhaps to hide, or maybe the people behind it didn't wish us be aware of the time. Evidently, someone was in control and leaked this type of information. Do you see this stain on the wall behind? You know what I'm talking about and take a look at the three dimensions of this in the face. It's fully frontal 3 dimension, just take a look at the face, this is amazing. The face, the skin is the main factor that tells you the fact that it's NOT CGI.

If I could create fake aliens with CGI similar to this I'd blur the image. Motion blur it to the point that it isn't obvious the fact that it's CGI since right here it is clear that this is real. is real.

Of course, someone who doesn't have any knowledge of CGI will be thinking, "Oh, that can be CGI." It's not, it cannot be CGI. You cannot simply take a frame of Avatar and turn it into black and white, and then create the illusion of real footage. The movements aren't quite right and it's not working that way. It's true that you can watch Avatar in black and white throughout the day and still be able to discern the real from the fake.

The thing is, CGI hasn't gotten to the point that it can fool people into thinking it's a complete representation of reality If it did been, our video games would be nearly virtual reality, but they aren't. I play the top video games and are aware that they're fantastic however, there's the look of a digital image; you will still get that cartoonish look even in the best of games. Even if they copy an actual photo of someone, and then convert the image digitally, it does not look like a real person. And making them black and white or blurring it won't make it look like a real person.

This is evident in the second footage of the fuzzy alien that was allegedly captured in Brazil. It's not like it fooled anyone, it was a joke. But I'm going to say that this is factual and I'm a huge fan of the show "Face-Off". Anyone who is familiar with Face-Off recognizes that the actors are truly top costume and anatomic builders. they are known for this type of things. However, if you take a look at the face, you won't see a stretchy eyelids blinking, holy shit look at this thing. take a look.

Screen captures using video footage of Grey Alien

I'd like you to take a an interest in something here. In the neck area, right beneath where you believe the ear is there's a little shape that it's a tendon or vein. I'd like you to pay particular focus on that particular region as you turn your head. is flexed, and I want you to notice how the skin as well as the shadowing moves and stretch.

If you could do this with CGI is the most stunning piece of CGI ever created now, as this piece of CGI could be the first to be realistic enough that it can fool someone to believe that it is real. If it's CGI I'm fooled, and this is my first experience to be happy to see an online game created out of this, because I could be transported to the game, and I'd wonder why I would make it all black and white? It could be colored, I'm sure that I'll put color into this game just to show you the color would be a good reason not to make it all black and white.

I would like you to be aware of places like this when the object moves, and look at it, and when you are looking closely enough, you'll realize that you're actually viewing a three-dimensional object, not a two-dimensional object that is trying to trick you into believing that it's. When you draw a 3 3-dimensional container on the chalkboard it's not actually three-dimensional It's flat.

It's drawn that way , and it's very similar to creating a 3-D image using the computer. The thing is, it's no longer a 3D image since the skin isn't stretched over it so it's not a 3-D image. In order to get that effect you must do programming for each specific area where the shadowing is stretched over by skin and that's the way I'm describing it.

It is interesting to see areas such as how the skinappears, how shadows move across it, all those small aspects and that's why I've zoomed into some of this footage so we can get some detail here and examine some of the things I'm talking about in this video. There isn't any debate about it. There is no question that this is footage.

If you're trying to argue about this then you'll have to make a claim that this is a form of mask, and you're going be required to present something like, "So and so designed an appearance that does this. You'll need to prove why each attempt to create fake alien videos does not even come close to this.

This is my belief as a key element of the "soft" disclosure that's been occurring over the past 3 or 4 years. The disclosure was made public in 2011, I believe, just ahead of 2012, but I may be mistaken. I would think that this might be released in 2012. It's true that Someone covered up some details such as making it in black-and-white. This flash is timed to ensure that you can tell that it's software that was designed for the purpose of duplicated both black and white. This is why they would like you to believe that the footage was more old that it actually is.

It is possible that someone has leaked the information to conceal their track. There could be a number of reasons for why they'd choose to make it black and white in order to hide the actual age. However is that we all recognize it's a fantastic option to hide the aging. It's a good thing, if were it not for tiny blip of color.

It seems like we're witnessing the first video footage of an alien being filmed and it's plausible to me, since we have skeletons, after all. It's the truth, those who don't believe this purely due to the subject is a bit narrow-minded due to the fact that we have human bodies of these beings that have DNA that states they are not aliens; they're not connected to any primate, but they have mitochondrial DNA that is human. Evidently, they kidnapped females around nine hundred years ago and injected them with their own species.

The final result, it demonstrates two things occurred nearly a century in the past. One Genetic manipulation was happening. Two, there were grays of about four feet with large heads and big eyes who snatched human females to bear their offspring. This was known in the past century, and thousands of people have reported this particular thing, and sure enough we see skulls.

This footage that appears real, and everyone's trying to convince themselves that "Well it's impossible to be real." What's the problem? Evidently, these things were floating all over the place. It is evident that at Roswell they crashed; witnesses saw the planes. Therefore, there's footage of these crashes.

The footage in question is truly amazing. What I'm thinking of in this video is it shows the alien at a table completing an jigsaw. It's like what the way they solve a puzzle for the same thing if they were a monkey. Assume a monkey is sitting down, and then hand it a small box that has a clover and triangular block. They place it into the hole. He moves it, turns his back to the table, he moves his arms, turns his head, looks back down , and then is looking up and smiling. It seems to me as if it's solving a problem really quickly, and then looking up at people and smiling.

The next one is just as amazing and is a full frontal profile. It's like the mugshot, but using footage. It's exactly what I would want the military to use in terms of documenting what a person appears to be. This is a stunning video This isn't an ad hominem it is a serious piece of evidence and I believe that ufology has to consider this extremely serious.

People should stop declaring, "this is CGI and not have the proof to claim that it's CGI. If you are able to make this, don't claim it's CGI. It's impossible for me to make it.

Here's the thing, perhaps Avatar is gorgeous and everything, but you're not capable of being able put two shades of black on Avatar and convince me that a single piece is actually real. If you can, good luck. I've never thought that a CGI UFO or CGI alien was real ever...never. Before I could consider an UFO image authentic, it must be backed by valid reports from MUFON the center for reporting and eyewitnesses. That's the kind of investigation I conduct I'm headed down to that volcano located in Mexico where UFOs are frequented on their official camera to check if there are witnesses to back these footage sightings.

So I don't believe in the footage I'm interested in knowing things and I've got enough knowledge of CGI to be able to tell that this footage isn't CGI in any way. The blinks aren't CGI. The tone of the muscle and the stretching of the skin over that muscle isn't CGI it's real footage, and I'm able to kind of see what's happening there. Of course , they've got the alien sitting at a desk. He works out a solution, is an intelligent rat smiling at the man and in the second, they show the frontal view.

Evidently, the alien submitted the full-frontal documentary footage and they are able to disclose it to the public. This is not to us and me but most likely to those responsible for this shit. However, this must be widely known. It is time to see the real thing and those who don't have the appropriate qualifications should stop stating that it's CGI. Also, other individuals who don't enjoy the show "Face-Off," who don't have a clue about the most effective Hollywood mask-making techniques need to stop saying that it could be anatomics, because you can see what they accomplish in the present. They're not able to make this stuff shit sorry."

I'm not sure what the source of evidence this commentator talking about when he talks about Skeletons and 900 years old genetic manipulation, but he appears to have a convincing argument to support the authenticity of the video. It would be fascinating to find out the possibility that a costume expert can make an appearance and recreate the kind of alien that is shown in the video.

One might wonder if the "grey" type of alien came out of actual experiences with aliens or the imagination of humans. When we imagine a vampire we envision fangs, and a hairstyle that is widow-peak When you think about Frankenstein and Frankenstein, we imagine lightning bolts around the neck and a head that is square and a huge body. Similar to that the classic 'grey' alien has become part of the culture thanks to its gray skin tone, almond-shaped eyes, and short height.

It's it's a relief to have the definitive proof of their existence, such as can be seen in the video above or some similar, or maybe something that is more certain.

Chapter 12: Ancient Alien Gods?

A brief program note

In the majority of the legends, myths and even the holy religious texts from all over the globe, there appears there is a common thread which suggest an intervention from the highest level. For sure, we aren't able to provide all of the answers. However, to depict every single mystery of the past as a possible encounter with aliens is an enormous injustice to the person reading. Overthinking it and finding evidence from ancient spacecrafts within each and every historical era would be the same as not considering the possibility of contact with aliens completely.

In the words of an aphorism that is often quoted, "It's good to have an open mind, but not so much that your brain is able to fall off!" And it is because of this reason -- to make sure to not lose mind that I've tried to provide this book a balanced blend of skepticism and creative speculation. Many an excellent old-fashioned astronaut theory has jumped into the depths by locating ancient aliens in locations that appear to be vanishingly impossible. The zealots then set about the creation of a new religion substituting the gods of mythology and popular religions with alien gods.

Before we start declaring that a astronaut who hails from Zeta Reticula as our newfound creator we should step back in order to prevent making the mistakes that ancient astronaut theorists say our predecessors made. In case we attempt to make aliens into gods all over again, we must remember that aliens couldn't be the ones to have created us any less that they might have made themselves. Contrary to what many would think that the theory of ancient astronauts is not a reason to dismiss the faith in God.

If you're a fan of God You can be a believer in the ancient theory of astronauts. The truth is that all matter in the universe - human, otherworldly, and all else in between came from the same source. Scientists believe that the universe was created as a tiny molecular that was exploded into existence about fourteen billion years back, in an event known as"the Big Bang. The molecule contained all the materials that would later be transformed into planets and stars, as well as all the other material which would later evolve into biological organisms living on distant planets across the universe that is ever-growing.

If you believe God intentionally triggered that Big Bang, that's fine If you believe that it happened in a random way, you're legally entitled to your belief too. But to repeat the error of Sumerians and the like. and make aliens gods that can accomplish such feats is absurd. According to Zachariah Sitchin that beings like Annunaki could have helped to shape man out of clay of the beginning but they did not make the Play-Doh!

Additional Reading and Reference
When you've reached the conclusion the book you might be interested in taking some time to look through the numerous

sources and references used in the writing process. It is your right to look through the entire collection.

Chariots from the Gods? Unsolved Mysteries of the Past. Erich Von Daniken

If you've ever read a book about the history of ancient astronauts, then you need to take a look at this book! The classic by Erich Von Daniken is the book that cracked the old astronaut theory and wide. Von Daniken is a great writer and has written a captivating story in his classic treatise on ancient astronauts. He is truly gifted in illustrating the complicated ideas he writes about and his views are convincing.

This is a blessing, as at the end of the day, the book is mostly composed of Von Daniken's views and speculations. Chariots of the Gods is an extremely entertaining read, however it reads more as an editorial instead of a research-based one. People who are reading the book from 1968 may be disappointed by the overly optimistic predictions about NASA's space programme. For instance the book makes the assumption that humanity will be able to establish a permanent lunar base by the time the 1980s come around!

Overall, though the book is an excellent reference for Ancient Astronaut theory. Zachariah Sitchin stunned the world with his interpretations of old Sumerian tablets. In these cuneiform inscriptions Sitchin claims to have discovered the full account of an expedition to the Earth that was carried out by the ancient astronauts. The collection of books in which he described this secret historical event The Earth Chronicles, and The End of Days is the seventh book and the final in the books in that series.

The book focuses on the supposed ET visitors as well as prophecies of global calamity prior to their return. This is a fascinating book that contains amazing information on the various legends, myths, and religious works that seem to be focusing on these issues. There are many excellent insights, however this book seems old-fashioned today: Sitchin makes a big statement about 2012 being a crucial year for a major shift.

The"official" Mayan prophecy of 2012 was nothing but a complete flop. The book was written in 2007, at a time when the 2012 the fever had reached its peak and Sitchin himself did not live to see his prophecy proven to be false. He passed away in the year the year 2010. So , we'll need to give the Sitchin a little slack, right?

Genesis Revisited Genesis Revisited: Is Modern Science Catching Up with Ancient Knowledge? Zachariah Sitchin

Sitchin was aware of the history of Near East very well, and in this book, he demonstrates this. Sitchin studies Genesis along with other older Near as well as Middle Eastern texts to analyze the possibility of a connection to technological developments in light of the information we are able to access in the present. Utilizing an ancient Sumerian Text as his reference, Sitchin questions whether the Genesis creation story Genesis was more complex than we imagined. It was complex enough to incorporate DNA manipulation, not less! He also discusses possible evidence that suggests a nuclear weapon could have been dropped onto the devastated cities of Sodom as well as Gomorrah. These are just a handful of the interesting examples of influences from the past of astronauts that Sitchin explores in his.

The Wars of Gods and Men. Zachariah Sitchin

In the third installment from the Sitchin's Earth Chronicles series, he investigates the possible connections between ancient wars and astronauts. Sitchin is thorough in this book. instead of merely reciting unsubstantiated speculation Sitchin backs up every one of his assertions with convincing evidence. This book is an excellent addition to any astronaut's library.

The Divine Encounters Book: A Comprehensive Guide to Visions as well as Angels as well as other Emissaries. Zachariah Sitchin

The book explores the role ancient astronauts served as guides and messengers in the past. They were often referred to as gods, angels or any other the entities were believed to be as sources of untold information. The book tells amazing stories of mankind's interactions with what he believed was the gods, and also what may be the ancient astronauts.

The Ancient Astronauts, Cosmic Collisions and other popular theories about man's past. William Stiebling

William Stiebling truly runs the range in this fascinating book that takes us on a journey with regard to the theories of the ancient astronaut. In this book, you'll discover every thought and theory that exists regarding possible ancient spacecraft communicating with the Earth. Though a lot of this has to be considered with a grain of salt however, the possibilities are interesting. If you're an historical astronaut fan You must read this book!

A Study of the Ancient Alien Question: A New Study of the Origins of Evidence, the Influence, and Evidence on Ancient Visitors. Philip Coppens

Like the long title suggests that this book is trying to present a new analysis of the theory of astronauts from the past. The book does this by looking at works of greatest scientists who preceded them, such as Erich Von Daniken and Carl Sagan. The author takes Sagan's assertion of Von Daniken basically ripped off the entire concept of an ancient astronaut from his.

Sagan did, as you may recall, make the baffling claim that Sagan was the person who sparked interest in ancient astronauts, even though he personally did not believe in the concept! Sagan's stance in the matter of ancient astronauts was similar to a chef who bakes cakes and insisting that they were the ones to credit however, he would later tell that people "Yeah that's what I did! However, it tastes awful!" And in fact Sagan's ambiguous view of ancient astronauts appears to be baked into from the beginning.

As the book by Philip Coppens relates, Sagan was often critical of the early astronaut theorists because they were not being sufficiently objective and for not expressing his understanding of the "speculative" characteristics of their work. Sagan was known to have a particular resentment to Von Daniken's Chariots of the Gods. According to what Coppens states, William Stiebling humorously refuted this assertion by asking "[Speculative? It's possible that Sagan did not realize over 230 questions in the book by Von Daniken!" Stiebling makes a excellent point, but at the same time , he himself could be seen as an overly enthusiastic supporter in the theory from Erich Von Daniken.

On the other hand, Coppens provides some much-needed information about the development for one of the biggest ground-breaking theories ever thought of. The book adds many new details to the earlier space-based theories and is aided by new developments in archeology, and indeed, science-based fact. Philip Coppens asks an incredible question and receives astonishing responses.

Passport to Magonia Passport to Magonia: A Guide to UFOs, Folklore, And Parallel Worlds. The Jacques Valleee

This book the renowned UFO researcher Jacques Vallee examines potential links between fairy tales from the past as well as the reports of alien intrusion that are happening in our present. There are many similarities in fairytale tales as well as alien interactions have been recognized by both skeptics as well as believers alike. Skeptics argue they can prove fairies and aliens are just myths transposed to a new setting. According to them, the entire UFO phenomenon is just an old-fashioned mythology, much like fairy tales existed prior to.

But not now Skeptics. If you believe in ancient astronauts instead of denying the UFO/alien phenomena of today, the similarities prove that alien involvement has been taking place for much longer than anybody could have ever imagined. According to Passport to Magonia suggests, maybe the fairy creatures of the past and the aliens of the present are the same.

Chapter 13: Ancient Annunaki Astronauts

It is impossible to start a discussion about ancient astronauts without discussing the mind-bending story of the Annunaki. The legends of the Annunaki "sky gods" who came down on humanity in the distant times come from the early Sumerians from Mesopotamia. Mesopotamia was situated in between Tigris and Euphrates and the name means "Land Between Rivers". Mesopotamian territory was comprised of portions of the present-day Syria, Iraq and Turkey.

Mesopotamia is the oldest known civilization, coming in the year 5500 BC. It was in Mesopotamia that we have an early example of mathematics, writing and astronomy. And it is the Sumerians have a unique understanding regarding the last that's caused the most curiosity and debate. Seven millennia ago, the Sumerians had a knowledge of the heavens which would never be replicated until the 19th century.

Recent research has shown that the inhabitants of ancient Mesopotamia were aware of the precise locations of the planets as well as small celestial bodies. There was no other ancient civilization that even was close to it. Indeed, at a point where the majority of people believed it was true that the Earth is flat, and the central point of the universe and that the universe was flat, the Sumerians were able to identify the sun as the central point of solar systems. They also effortlessly identified all of the satellites and planets which revolve around it.

In addition they also provided vivid descriptions of the color patterns that appear on the surface of these distant worlds. The Cuneiform tablets from Mesopotamia the detailed explanations about Uranus and Neptune have been found. While archeologists have been wondered about the illogical information possessed by the Sumerians and their people, the way in which a culture who did not have telescopes had this kind of information has not been fully explained.

However, should we inquire of the Sumerians themselves, or rather, look up the writings they left on their clay tablets -- we might be educated. As per the late researcher, writer and the proponent of ancient astronauts Zachariah S. Sitchin, if you look through the cuneiform records and find a way to penetrate the mystery surrounding the early Mesopotamian civilization. This is precisely that Sitchin did.

Sitchin who is from the Central Asian country of Azerbaijan moved in America. United States in the early 1950s. Being familiar in Hebrew as well as other old Semitic languages and cultures, he decided to improve his Cuneiform as a supervisor for an unnamed shipping company located in New York City. It was possible that he earned an income as a logistics specialist however his real love of language was always his, and soon he was proficient in the ancient language of Sumerian. After decades of studying and research, he put together his findings into the cult ancient astronaut workbook The 12th Planet. In the book, Sitchin says he's found an unsettling account of the ancient alien intrusion into the lives of humans.

Sitchin's fascination with the intriguing possibility of alien contact started when he was just a kid watching an Rabbi read Hebrew texts. Sitchin was intrigued by an obscure passage in Genesis. Book of Genesis that describes angels coming down to Earth and interspersed with humankind.

In the Bible the beings mentioned along with their descendants are referred to as Nephilim. Nephilim are Hebrew definition of the term is "those who were cast down". Based on the information in the Bible says (and we'll look at some possible biblical stories of ancient astronauts later) They have been sent back to Earth to oversee the human race (other texts refer to Nephilim as the "Watchers"). They were believed to be mandated to keep watch over the progress of humanity, but they were not permitted to communicate or interfere in humans' daily lives.

In the Bible the Bible, these creatures refused to obey their orders and started to talk to human beings. Then, it declares that they discovered the "daughters of man beautiful" they decided that it was a good idea to mix with them! It is evident that God was not happy with this beautiful hanky-panky and swiftly ended the affair. The tale is disturbing to not the least, but after these awe-inspiring passages it is clear that the Bible is mostly silent on the incredible incident.

The tale remained in Sitchin's head for a long time however, it came out of the ashes when Sitchin began studying the ancient Sumerian cuneiform. Surprisingly Sitchin discovered stories of all-too similar encounters written by the clay tablet. Most notable among them is that Sumerian mythology recounts the tale of the Annunaki 200 celestial beings that came down to Earth and started to influence the world. Incredibly enough, the long-lost Biblical Book of Enoch, only discovered at the end of the 18th century specifically mentions that they were an exact 200 angels that "left their home" of heaven to bring mischief to Earth.

Sitchin began to notice interesting similarities everywhere he went at, but it was the Sumerian account of the events that he came across the most precise explanation for who the Nephilim he had learned from Torah school actually were. According to Sitchin an ancient Sumerian text indicates how the Annunaki or Nephilim are astronauts who were brought to Earth from a planet at the outer edge of the solar system, called Niburu with a purpose to extract gold.

They weren't looking to create exquisite jewelry. According to Sitchin states that the ancient astronauts required gold to survive. Because Niburu is so distant away from sunlight, planet depended on a very thick and dense atmosphere to keep the heat. But due to pollution as well as natural disasters and perhaps an nuclear conflict, planet's climate was starting to shrink. Based on the information Sitchin learned out of the clay tablet the answer that Annunaki found to solve their problem was the development of a shield that absorbed heat from the planet comprised with fine silver particles.

Unfortunately, Niburu had long since diminished its gold reserves and it was that the ancient astronauts arrived on Earth to mine this essential resource. The tablets described the 200 Annunaki astronauts who left their home planet for a journey to the third planet , which is located away from the Sun. Sitchin believes that archeological evidence exists of an Annunaki mine operation located in the Persian Gulf, and another in Southeast Africa, going back up to the 400,000th year in the past.

The story becomes more complex. It is believed that these extraterrestrials who lived for a long time worked tirelessly for around 100,000 years until the Annunaki who were that were assigned to their work became tired of their job and rebelled against their bosses. With their usual crews in strike they began looking for work elsewhere and the best applicants were primitive humans they met.

But, the early human species weren't as advanced as women and men are nowadays. To be efficient, the Annunaki had to give genetics of humans an early start with splicing their genetic material our own. So, the Sumerian text discusses the same interbreeding between human and alien species like does the Book of Genesis does with the inclusion of Nephilim. However, in contrast to the Bible's romantic tale of angels falling in romantic connections with humans and humans, the Sumerian text is a more scientific and scientific process performed in a laboratory.

Sitchin states that the text identifies one of the initial genetically engineered humans as "Adamah". It's hard not to see the resemblance between Adamah and Adam, the biblical first man Adam however, these early humans weren't created from dirt but instead of mixed genetic material in test tubes. Sitchin describes the process as similar as modern-day in vitro fertilization and states that the procedure is explained in detail on various Sumerian clay tablet.

He even cites quite convincing drawings that were found in Mesopotamia as evidence. The ancient art depicts Annunaki with objects in their possession that appear quite similar to glass testing tubes. A third being is believed to be presenting a baby--a fresh living, breathing humanoid creature as the outcome of their experiments--to the other.

If we were to believe the writings of the ancient Sumerians literally, our modern-day humanity can be traced to ancient spacecrafts "playing God"(as Sitchin puts it) by combining our DNA. To be precise, Sitchin does not believe that the beings they portrayed were gods, nor at all god-like. Sitchin believes they were flesh-and-blood humanoids similar to us. They just had technological advancements that allowed them to profit from the possibility of manipulating our DNA. In this way it isn't like the Annunaki created humanity in the same way that they invented themselves. They used what was already in existence--a primitive ape-man, and applied their knowledge in genetic engineering design an entirely new and improved version.

Sitchin believes his theory that the Niburu species as well as Earth have been "genetically compatible" since the beginning, and that permitted cross-breeding between the two species to occur. He argues it is"the "seed for life" that allowed the Annunaki to grow in their own Earth was the same genetic spark that is present on Earth. Although the Annunaki were at the advanced stages and shared DNA, it let their scientists see the potential of humanity and they decided to kick-start the development of DNA from humans.

According to Sitchin Human beings would have evolved naturally similar to the way they did without Annunaki's influence, but over a much longer amount of time. The only thing Annunaki could do was speed up the process. Not god-like beings infusing life into clay, these ancient astronauts were adept geneticists who controlled humans' genomes. Of course, this is apparent when viewed through the lens of contemporary knowledge. Even if the ancient Sumerians, even if the Annunaki themselves attempted to dissuade them, no doubt they would have maintained that the gods that descended from the heavens were gods.

According to Sitchin's interpretation his interpretation, the Sumerian story is a reference to two most renowned Annunaki geneticists: Enki and Ninti. It is interesting to note that, in addition to being research collaborators who conducted numerous experiments, these two scientists are also believed to be lovers! Ninti describes herself as a gorgeous Annunaki female who is being romantically linked to the leading scientist, a male Annunaki known as Enki.

The Sumerian texts explain the Annunaki who were stationed in Earth and far from their homelands, often found themselves bored and with lots of time their hands. When they had time off they were engaged in the same relationships outside of school which bored humans today would. Since Enki as well as Ninti working in the same outpost, conducting the same boring study in the exact same labs, romance was inevitable.

The Sumerian text captures the entire story in complete details. In a few passages, the Annunaki couple appear to be a bit sly and create bizarre humanoids to have fun. One time, they create a human genetically without sexual organs. In another case, their research led to a person who "could not contain the odor of his urine". It's like Annunaki lovers Enki and Ninti created a person who had urinary incontinence so they could have something fun to discuss during lunch break in the laboratory!

In one chapter, Ninti is even shown smiling jokingly about the bizarreities produced: "How good or bad is the human body? When my heart tells me, I will change its fate to favorable or unfavorable!" (Cue canned Annunaki laughter.) If we take the word of these interpretations of Sumerian cuneiform tabletsfrom the beginning, man was in the midst of the whimsy of a variety of alien beings who used him , not only as a guinea fowl but also as the dart of their farts!

However, eventually, Enki and Ninti buckled into business they perfected their methods and were able to create humans for the very first time. Humans were created to resemble the Annunaki in every regard: their life span. In contrast to those who were long lived Annunaki "a single day seemed as long as 1000 years" humans were deliberately designed for shorter duration. In contrast to this shorter duration was the capacity granted to mankind to "be prosperous and multiply"--which rapidly led to the creation of a massive population to mine gold.

No, instead of relaxing in the idyllic Garden of Eden, these first Adams and Eaves were sent to work tough work within the mining operations for the precious metals! Their only goal in their lives was to find gold-rich reserves for Annunaki's taskmasters. Do you think it is because of this that all people around the world have it etched into their minds that gold is precious? Did this notion of the worth of gold embedded in our collective memory from the agonizing labor that humanity endured in the Annunaki's mines?

In the subsequent tens of thousands of years, humanity gathered huge amounts of this valuable resource to serve their alien masters however, the Annunaki eventually were tired of their creation. Based on the Sumerian mythology that is the basis of Gilgamesh's Epic of Gilgamesh, the Annunaki chose to eliminate humanity and begin all over again. Sitchin's interpretation of Sumerian texts indicates that the Annunaki initiated a campaign of extermination passively by taking away vital aid from people. Food supplies were scarce and many people starved, however humanity proved to be more resilient than the Annunaki were aware of and the human race as a whole was not in danger of dying.

Fortunately the Annunaki were given another possibility of man's destruction by scientists aboard a spacecraft orbiting discovered gravity pull of the next passage of Niburu will pull on the glaciers of the Earth enough to cause them slide to the sea, elevating the level of the ocean and causing the possibility of a global flood. The Annunaki believed that the catastrophe would end the world without lifting the finger (or the equivalent of a digit could find). All they needed to do was keep the issue to themselves and wait for a watery Armageddon.

As it transpired, the principal scientist behind the project was not willing to let his coveted creation go to waste. So he defied his orders and came up with a way to save a few human specimens. Based on Sitchin, Enki created a special submersible vessel where people he hand-picked would like to see survive the disaster. In this ark that resembled a submarine the lucky people were able to survive the deluge that killed their entire kin.

Prior to the flooding The Annunaki on the Earth evacuated and climbed on their "chariots" to climb to the skies. The Annunaki stood by the flood from their spacecrafts, circling the planet , watching the waves spread across the Earth. Once the waters receded, they returned to the atmosphere of Earth and landed on the top of the Turkish Mount Ararat.

In line with the biblical story the human people who survived the flooding were able to land in their own vessel of protection here too. Enki was scolded for his conduct after it was revealed that he was able to spare only a handful of rare humans However, at the final, he managed persuade his bosses that it was important for him to have a handful of human beings around for the duration of time.

It is evident--and again, this is tied to the biblical story--that the main complaint about"the human program "human programme" was that the Annunaki were indeed finding the daughters (and even their sons) of men to be fair, and had begun interbreeding with the Annunaki. This destroyed the ideal metric of a human's short life span, as the children from these unions ended up living much longer than an average human being could. Annunaki high command was worried about the possibility that these upstarts with long lives would grow too fast for them to manage and they had slated them for destruction.

Based on the Sumerian story, they'd been correct to be concerned. With a shorter lifespan the descendants of victims of the Flood started to stir up a ruckus at Annunaki headquarters again. It was simply because they were being too intelligent for their own good. Sitchin refers to an Sumerian story that echoes what many people are familiar with to be the Biblical "Tower of Babel" story , which is another Annunaki attempt to impede the development of mankind.

The Bible tells us about the Land of Shin'ar, in which the people of that time gathered in the city of Babylon with the intention of creating an edifice "whose head would rise to the sky". There's a similar Sumerian equivalent to this tale however Sitchin insists that the Sumerian story reveals more about the things that ancient Babylonians were doing. According to Sitchin the

Babylonians weren't just creating a tall building built of bricks. They constructed the launch pad that they could launch missiles in space!

The Annunaki leadership decided that humans, despite their shorter lifespan have become too clever to be a good thing for themselves, so these astronauts of the past employed the classic divide-and-conquer strategy. Humans were initially speaking the same language, however the Annunaki changed their programming to speak a variety of languages to slow the pace of technological advancement. It appeared that if early humans were working together, they were able to accomplish anything, and so they did. It was because the Annunaki intentionally misinterpreted their tongues, bringing their cooperation to a screeching stop.

After having read the myriad of fantasies and wild tales What are we to think of the Annunaki astronauts from the past? Do these stories simply reflect the work of an old Sumerian's hyperactive imagination? Or are they evidence from eyewitnesses of not just contact with aliens as well as alien interference in all levels of human development? Zachariah Sitchin died in 2010but a lot of his work is being considered. The only way to know is the extent to which his assertions about antiquated Annunaki astronauts actually were.

The ancient Astronauts from the Bible

A lot of the Scripture's most dramatic descriptions of possible encounters with astronauts from the past were previously described within the preceding chapter and in order to avoid repetition, we'll just touch on the stories briefly. As we've discussed before One of the most debated of these claims of encounters involves the Nephilim. A lot of people believe the Nephilim from the Bible as well as that of Annunaki of Sumerian mythology are the same entities. From a biblical perspective however, they are typically depicted as angels descending into the Earth who break the rules of God by mingling with humans.

Only a handful of specific mentions of these enigmatic beings in the standard canon Bible. There is a brief mention of them in the Book of Genesis, a reference in a passage in the Book of Numbers, and brief descriptions within the Book of Jude in the New Testament. It is the Book of Jude, which provides a detailed account of the way in which Nephilim "left their original home" of heaven to be a part of humanity in the present, is actually a reference to the mythical Book of Enoch. While Enoch's Book of Enoch is not an official part of the biblical canon today but it was at one time.

The decision to leave it out was made in 381 AD in the Council of Laodicea. Theologians of the time believed that Enoch's bizarre tales of angels interbreeding with human beings somewhat too fantastical to believein, and they decided to leave the publication out of future version of the Bible. A majority of the mainline churches followed this dictum, and a large portion documents of this text fell to dust throughout the centuries. Then, in 1773, an archeologist who was part-time or full-time adventurer Scottish explorationist James Bruce, found a copy of the long-lost book completely intact, hidden in the monastery of Ethiopia and then unveiled details of the text to contemporary world.

The Book of Enoch picks up from where the mysterious passages concerning The Nephilim from the Book of Genesis leave off. Nearly word-for-word it is the Book of Enoch echoes, "And it happened that the number of men's sons were growing and increased, they were blessed with beautiful and pretty daughters. And the Angels also, the children of Heaven were able to see them and admired them. They also told one another "Come and let us pick to be our own wives, among the men's children, and let us make our own children."

Let's first be aware it is that Book of Enoch attempts to identify who the Sons from Heaven were. The Book of Enoch explicitly describes them as angels, as opposed to the scriptures of Genesis only leave us with the phrase "sons of God". But The Book of Enoch goes further in its descriptions of the entities, and goes much more. Since right after these echos of Genesis We are flooded with specific descriptions of these creatures and their activities, beginning with the leader for the group.

The Book of Enoch tells us, "And Semyaza, who was their leader, told them, 'I am afraid that you might not wish for this act to happen and that only I will be the one to pay for this terrible sin. They all listened to him and they said, "Let us all swear an oath and tie each other with curses to ensure that we do not change this plan, but instead execute this plan in a timely manner."

The goal, as per Enoch is that they would descend into Earth and cross-breed with human beings. What is the reason these celestial beings arrive on Earth in order to enjoy enjoyment from Earth women? For many, it appears that something that is missing from the tale Enoch tells. For instance, as has been mentioned, the an ancient Near East scholar Zachariah Sitchin believes that the events were intentional genetic manipulation.

While staying true to the story that is told through Enoch's Book of Enoch, these 200 supernatural beings emerged from the mountain in ten-strong bands, seeking women to become their wives. In addition to having a sexual relationship with these women, angels taught them specific spells and charms and advanced astronomy and other technology developments that they were not allowed to reveal.

The mother later gave their angelic offspring who were half-human, half-angel children proved difficult to control. It is said in the Book of Enoch states that these children, gifted with the power of angels they relentlessly "devoured all the struggles of men until the men could not support their own power". After this harrowing situation is revealed, the narrative is cut to a picture of four Archangels Michael, Gabriel, Suriel as well as Uriel "looking towards Heaven" while discussing the destruction caused by their rebellious brothers.

They acknowledge that the situation is so bad that the very souls of men are "complaining"--apparently, even the bodiless souls were crying out, "Bring our complaint before the Most High!" Or, as the Book of Enoch describes it, "And now behold the souls which have died cry out and complain unto the Gate of Heaven, and their lament has ascended, and they cannot go out in the face of the iniquity which is being committed on the Earth."

The Book of Enoch goes on to explain it was the case that Most Exalted sent an angel known as Arsyalayur in the direction of"the "son of Lamech"--which according to the Bible was Noah. The angel directed him to give the following important message: "Say to him in My name: Go away! Then show him the time of the end that is about to occur, since the entire Earth is going to be destroyed. A deluge is set to hit the entire Earth and everything of the Earth will go to waste. Learn to teach him now so to escape, and his descendants may live for the entire Earth." The story of a carefully selected group of people who are spared from a massive flood obviously, aligns with the biblical flood story as well as The Sumerian legend.

Before we get into the Enoch version of the story It is crucial to take note of earlier passages in the Book of Enoch which introduce Noah's mysterious background. Enoch mentions Noah's father Lamech as being frightened and perplexed after he realizes that there's something unusual about Noah's appearance. His hair is of a pale hue and his eyes and skin are glowing with a strange glow that is literally making the room glow.

Inquiring about the reason Noah's father was worried. Lamech called his dad, Methuselah and in return, consulted his very own old father, Enoch. In the course of this game of telephone from the Bible, Enoch informed Methuselah that the boy's unusual appearance was the will of God. Also, he instructed Methuselah to explain to

Lamech, "that the one who was born is really his son. Also, he should call him Noah because Noah will be a relic for you along with his brothers will be spared from the destruction that is coming to the Earth due to all the sins and the wrongs that will be committed on Earth in the days to come."

After the reveal of the role Noah was to be playing, Enoch goes on to explain how celestial beings revealed more to Noah. (It could be interesting to the contemporary person who reads this story to learn that Enoch declares that the entities gave their information to him via "tablets that came from Heaven". Tablets that belong to Heaven? We can definitely enjoy a good laugh old Enoch's jokes when we imagine ancient astronauts writing their instructions to him (on the other side of the galaxy (similar to Microsoft Touch!)

It is not clear what these tablets actually were but the essence about what Enoch was told was "generation after generation" of humanity would "do wrong" until the "generation of righteousness will emerge".

A few ancient astronaut theorists believe that this refers to genetic manipulation, which will eventually lead to an idealized generation, however obviously the more popular theory is that it refers to the condition of the soul, not his DNA. However, Enoch was informed that the responsibility was on Noah who's name is translated to "remnant" to protect the humanity that was left.

The next episode in the biblical story which could be thought of as a meeting with the ancient astronauts takes place further from the Book of Genesis. It concerns Lot, the patriarch of biblical times. Lot. Lot lived in the ruined city of Sodom that was scheduled for destruction by God because its people were extremely sinful.

But prior to the day of judgement, God sent down his personal emissaries who were sent to carry out one final fact-finding trip as and to also warn Lot that he was about the only decent man left in the town. Lot was enjoying his time in the gates of the city of Sodom when he spotted two mysterious entities advancing towards him. The Bible does not specify what they looked like, but it's evident from Lot's response that he quickly realized they weren't your typical people who visited Sodom. The moment he was aware of the people, Lot put on his best smile, addressed the people, and demanded that they let him enjoy the traditional Middle Eastern hospitality.

This is fascinating, as often when angels are mentioned within the Bible they are instantly overcome by fear. In almost every other Biblical account about angels, the very first thing that the angel is required to tell the angel"do not be afraid "do not be scared". In addition to his eagerness to please his guest, Lot did not seem at all scared of them. As things would later reveal, no one other than Sodom was particularly scared of them either.

In actual fact the moment that Lot's neighbors found out that he was hosting to a few extraterrestrial beings, instead being terrified they became incredulous and demanded access to the guests! It appears that, regardless of the reason, inhabitants of Sodom were familiar with such encounters, and even actively sought for them. As the night progressed, Lot's neighbors, seemingly feeling that they had missed from the excitement were encircling his home and began shouting out demands, such as "Where were the people that arrived at your door this evening? Bring them for us so in order that we can meet the men."

Later theologians have generally believed that the depraved inhabitants from Sodom spoke in a biblical sense and wanting to have sexual relations with angels (although there are several theories). However, whatever the reason is the fact remains that when Lot was unable to present his angels who were visiting him to the people The petty group tried to slash his door. The beings intervened by making the crowd blind. According to the Bible the beings "smote the people in the front of the house by blindness, old and young; and they wore themselves out trying to locate the entrance."

Their attack had appeared to be enough to make the angels come to a decision however, and they decided that Sodom must be destroyed. When they turned to Lot and his family, they told him "Who else is there besides a son-in law as well as thy daughters and sons and other relatives that are living in the city, bring them out of this city because we're going to destroy the city."

When Lot informed his son-in-law of the incident on the following day, the next day, he was however met by a raucous laughter. that's why it was just Lot and his wife and his daughters who were not married who left Sodom. Soon after Lot was removed from his danger area, Sodom, along with the city that was adjacent to it, Gomorrah was totally destroyed. The Bible says, "Then the Lord rained on Sodom and Gomorrah the brimstone and fire of the Lord from heaven. Then he smashed them down as well as the whole plain as well as all the inhabitants of the cities, as well as all that grew on the surface."

Many have drawn attention to the strange similarities between the biblical story as well as a nuclear blast. Nuclear explosions are in fact the only thing that we've seen that could destroy a city completely to the ground and destroy all evidence of vegetation. Another intriguing part of the story is the dire warning issued by angels "not to look behind". Perhaps, the wife of Lot who was emotional about leaving their beloved city, did look back, however. The result was that she was transformed into the form of a salt pillar, or according to some translations it as vapour. Also Lot's wife went through a process of vaporization!

What strange surge of energy can cause such an event? Was it truly the divine will of God or was it simply the weapons of the ancient astronauts? If ancient astronauts were tampering with humankind then why would they decided to do it? destruction to old Neolithic cities using nuclear bombs?

Jacob, the biblical patriarch Jacob experienced a less deadly meeting with an enigmatic entity however, it was nevertheless a complete mystery. The incident occurred when Jacob was crossing the Jordan late at night to get back to the country of Canaan from a cross-country trek to Harran. His journey was interrupted by an unidentified man who was blocking his way. Jacob began wrestling with the entity and the fight was so intense that it continued until dawn. It wasn't until the end of the match did Jacob realise that it wasn't the man that he was wrestling with but was an heavenly being. Then, Jacob called the site of his match "Peni-El" or, for that matter "the Face of God".

Jacob had a different interesting experience to look forward to prior to his return home. It was still late in the night, so Jacob chose to take a break and take a rest. When he woke up, the next thing he knew, he woke up to flashing lights. He also saw above him a mysterious vehicle with a ladder coming down from an open door to the ground. The ladder that was ascending and descended were creatures that Jacob believed were the divine host.

Theorists of the past point to Jacob's ladder as a definite evidence of the ancient alien's visitation. The theory is that the blinking, moving object Jacob observed was a UFO equipped with ramps that aliens were moving into and out.

To better get their point of view We can simply take Jacob's story and place it in an actual setting. Consider, for instance, an unassuming young man out who is on a hike, telling the exact same story. Even those who do not believe in UFOs would likely conclude that an UFO encounter was the one that the young hiker was talking about. For instance, if someone claims that they fell asleep in the woods only to wake up to an object that had flashing lights hovering over them. Cue the X-Files theme tune on our minds! Even if we believed that the entire story up, we'd instantly realize that he was inventing the story of the appearance of some alien-like craft.

Why is it that we do not have similar reactions when hear about exactly the same type of sighting in stories like Jacob's ladder? This kind of questioning that started most of the curiosity about the concept of ancient astronauts in the first place.

Following Jacob the next biblical figure some believe was visited by the ancient astronauts is his patriarch Moses. To provide a some background to the story, keep in mind this: Moses was the child of Hebrew slaves who were accepted into his parents, the Egyptian Royal family. He was elevated to the rank of a government official however, one day he observed an Egyptian overseer brutally murder an innocent Hebrew slave. Moses was furious and screamed without thought and killed the overseer. Then he fled into the desert to avoid the negative consequences.

In the course of hiding in the desert, he stumbled upon Mt. Horeb which is known as the "Mountain of God", and it was at this point that the man came across a mysterious glowing object that was described by him as the "burning Bush". Moses identified a bush which was ablaze with an intense brightness, but somehow not completely consumed however, the proponents of ancient astronauts claim that it was an object of technology. The light, they argue was either due to the intense artificial light or the use of a more sophisticated technology like a protection force field.

The Bible says that when Moses was looking at the burning bush, he heard the sound of a voice coming from it that gave the order "Do not approach any further." Moses froze in his tracks and gazed at the bizarre sight before him , as it instructed, "Take off your sandals because the ground on which you stand has been declared holy." This bush declared, "I am the God of your grandparents and the God of Abraham and Isaac, God of Isaac, the God of Isaac and the God of Jacob." The burning bush therefore displayed an intimate understanding of Moses his genealogy and was usually extremely important in the early Middle East.

The voice continued to state that it was deeply worried about the way in which Hebrew people were taken care of in Egypt. Moses was informed that the Hebrews would be saved and taken out of Egypt to the new "land filled with honey and milk" where they would live in peace and peace. The entity also instructed Moses to go back to Egypt to serve as the messenger of this news. Moses was stunned however, he was still wary when faced with the enormity of the task at hand He began to hesitate.

He was fumbling for time and demanded the burning bush to, "Suppose I go to the Israelites and tell them "The God who sent you your fathers and they then ask me, 'What's the name of his God? And what should I say to you?" To this the burning bush responded, "I AM who I am. What are you to tell the Israelites"I AM sent me to you.'"

Theologians and scholars have thought on this concept since. For the more metaphysically inclined in our society, such statement directly from the eternal God that has no beginning or ending is logical. According to them, God is revealing a amazing secret about the inner processes of this universe. What is the origin of God originate from? Who was the one who created God? Nobody knows. God exists because he wants to be! As the burning bush said, "I AM who I am".

Judaism is also affected by this particular detail of Moses meeting at the time of burning the bush. Because the moment that Moses demanded of God to reveal his identity, Moses was told that God was just "I Am", Jews traditionally believe that God's name is far too sacred to be even spoken of. Moses also had a second encounter with God or an ancient astronaut, based on your viewpoint--while in charge of leading his Hebrew group to freedom from Egypt. We've all heard the tale of Moses lifting his staff to the waters which kept those Hebrews from freedom and how they were separated from the Red Sea parted before the mass of people. However, many people do not realize that a mysterious, bright object was hovering above the sea at precisely the same time. A lot of the theories about ancient astronauts hold that the sea broke up not due to Moses raised his staff instead, a spacecraft that was hovering used the electromagnetic force or gravitational field to divide the sea and provide a route of dry terrain to the Israelites to follow in their escape.

The craft would be a prominent part of the Exodus story, as it led to lead the Hebrews throughout the wilds. The -for absence of a better term--UFO was a bright cloud (perhaps saucer-shaped) in the daytime and also as a pillar of fire (maybe lit with flashing lights) in the night. This was so brilliant that Hebrews could easily walk through the darkness of nighttime desert by lighting its way. Numerous miracles were believed to be due to this particular object like the making of a healthy food the Hebrews called Manna, which is a bread that came from heaven. The bread would pour down from the craft and hungry Hebrews would leave and take it home in baskets, then take it in for the rest of the day.

The interesting thing is to know that the object that hovers is often referred to as a cloud during the daytime sightings. Through the entire Bible airborne anomalies are frequently called clouds. Most of the time, the reference is the typical rain cloud, however in other cases, these cloud-like phenomena are evidently something completely different. For instance, if the Bible states that somebody was "taken by the air" with a cloud it's certainly not talking about the phenomenon of meteorology!

"Cloud" of Exodus "cloud" was not able to limit itself to hovering over the Israelites while they walked throughout the wilds. Sometimes, it would be seen landing on Mt. Sinai for private talks with Moses. The biblical account is ambiguous about the specifics of the events that occurred during the meeting between Moses and the clouds. often, we're only given an idea of what Moses was looking like when he ascended from Mount Sinai. In the famous story the time he returned to his camp bearing the ten commandments inscribed on stone tablets for instance, we learn that Moses's facial features were "lit with the light of the sun" while his body was glowing with an unnatural glowing. What is this indicating? Numerous ancient astronauts have proposed Moses's skin was glowing due to exposure to some kind or intense radiation.

Another biblical figure who experienced thrilling encounters with strange celestial objects was the prophet Ezekiel. Ezekiel was in the region known as Harran, the same area from which Jacob returned to wrestle the angel. He was on the bank of the Khabur River when he saw an astonishing sight. It was the appearance of a sudden "whirlwind" that Ezekiel was confronted by strange objects that flashed lights. Ezekiel also describes the object as an "great cloud that had a raging flames engulfing it; and the brightness was everywhere and radiating out from its center as if it were amber". As I previously mentioned, the language for describing strange aerial phenomena was not as extensive in the days of Ezekiel. Moreover, the Bible describes all kinds of huge moving items as clouds. In order to know the exact nature of what Ezekiel tried to convey his vision, I will read his story in all its entirety:

And I sat and then the whirlwind appeared from the north, a huge cloud, with a flame that was enfolding itself, and a luminosity was around it. It emerged from its midst was the hue of amber in the midst the flame. Out of the midst of the fire was the appearance of four living things. They had this appearance. They had the appearance of men. Every one of them had four faces and each had four wings. Their feet were straight; and the soles of their feet were similar to an ox's feet They sparkled as the burnished brass color. They were armed like an individual on their four sides, and they had four faces and wings. The wings of their wings were joined one to the other and they did not turn when they flew; they were all straight forward. For the resemblance in their appearance, four had the appearance of an ox, on the left; they also were adorned with the face of an Eagle. They had the same faces Their wings stretched upwards; the wings of each were joined to one another and two were covered over their bodies. And they walked straight ahead: wherever the spirit was supposed to go they went, and they didn't turn back to turn back when they left. In terms of the resemblance to living creatures Their appearance was that of glowing fire coals as well as their appearance as lamps. they moved between the living creatures. the flame was glowing and from the flame came lightning. And the living creatures sped off back and came back as the look of of lightning. As I looked at those living beings, I saw one wheel on the earth created by living creatures, and his four faces. Their appearance wheels as well as their work were similar to beryl's color They all had a similarity, and their appearance and work were like one wheel within the middle of an elongated wheel. When they left to the road, they went on their four sides; They did not turn when they moved. In regard to the rings they were so tall that they were terrifying Their rings had eyes around them. When the living creatures moved through the earth, the wheels followed them. And when they were raised from the earth then their wheels were raised. Wherever the spirit wanted in motion, and they left. where was their spirit's desire to go. And the wheels were raised up against them. For that spirit was within the wheels. When they went, these moved; and when they were standing, they stood. and when they were lifted from the ground the wheels were lifted to the sky over them, because their spirit, which was living and immortality was contained in the wheels. The resemblance of the firmament that was on the head of living creatures was like the hue of the horrible crystal that was stretched out above their heads.

Four wings and faces of creatures that shimmered like bronze that has been burned? What do you think Ezekiel discussing? According to the proponents of the ancient theory of the astronaut, Ezekiel was logging an eyewitness report of the landing an unidentified spacecraft! According to this interpretation of events"the "whirlwind" signified the entrance of the spacecraft into earth's atmosphere. "The "great cloud" was the vehicle itself and the "fire that was enfolding it" along with its "brightness" it could be seen "about it" it is understood as some kind of shielding force field, which is "the colour of the amber" and visible to any naked eyes. The larger craft, emerged four smaller scout vessels that Ezekiel with his limited knowledge could only discern as "four life-forms".

You probably would not mistake an airplane for the animal that it is, yet it is important to recognize that Ezekiel was alive before the invention of any type of mechanical transport. To him, everything moving was living. If you could go back in time and drive a car driven by old Ezekiel and his family, you will surely conclude you're Honda Civic was a living creature since it moved!

147

Additionally, Ezekiel observed that the "four living creatures" had straight legs. It is the oldest astronaut belief that the "legs" are actually land gears or shock absorbers to the craft.

Ezekiel later describes the landing of the craft as well as the rise of the four passengers. The scribe says that the creatures possessed human-like characteristics. In other words, they were humanoid and had two legs as well as two arms and a head. Yet, the mystery is that Ezekiel also states that they were "four faces". People who believe in the old astronaut theory are of the opinion that this was the result of Ezekiel's inexperienced attempt to clarify the head gear the creatures were wearing. The four face faces could been different lenses on the creature's protective helmets? Similar to when Ezekiel mentions wheels that are ringed with eyes, could the eyes be flashing lights? What was Ezekiel actually observe? Was it a vision from God or of the extraterrestrial?

It's fascinating to consider that the sighting of Ezekiel was triggered by the appearance of the appearance of a "whirlwind" (or energy vortex) in the horizon. This is because it was the same time that another prominent historical patriarch of the Bible, Elijah as well as his pupil Elisha were experiencing the exact similar incident. The Bible tells us that "And it transpired that while they [Elijah and Elishawere still talking and talked they saw an erupting chariot of fire and fire-breathing horses and split them into two pieces and Elijah was carried up in the whirlwind and went to heaven."

The "chariot filled with fire" which Elijah ascensated was an alien spacecraft, the "whirlwind" could be the cause of the disturbance when it entered and left the air. As for Elijah himself who was never seen again, can we claim that Elijah was the very first as a victim of alien abduction? Like most cases in this particular subject the answer is dependent on the person you speak to and, in any event, there are many who believe they are of the opinion that visions from the Old Testament patriarchs are too filled with symbolism and double significance to be credible eyewitness evidence.

If it is true that the Old Testament is too remote for those who doubt it, could it be possible to prove that the New Testament be any more convincing? It turns out that it is the New Testament has one of the Bible's most intriguing stories of a mysterious flying object. And it is right at the beginning. The very first book of the New Testament is the Book of Mathew It is in this book that we learn the tale about the Star of Bethlehem. In this narrative there are three "Magi" also known as "Wise men" who hail from the East discover an unusual sky-like star, and they discover that a King has been born.

From a first impression, it appears to be something more than the science of astrology. Reading astrological horoscopes or casting horoscopes charts was, in fact an everyday pastime for "wise men" during the time. However, the Magi weren't just watching the star, but actively studying the direction it was taking. This star was reportedly mobile. Modern science of astronomy has shown the concept that stars are suns that remain in their place and are unable to be moved across the sky. We can therefore conclude that the celestial object in question was not an actual "star" as defined in the usual sense.

It is possible, as some have claimed that the object the Magi described as an astronomical star actually was the comet. Comets are bright, luminous objects that actually traverse the sky regularly. Comets can also be an important sign for any aspiring astrologer because comets were believed to be associated with significant occasions, such as that of the birth of the King. Therefore, the notion about being the Star of Bethlehem being a comet is fitting the story quite perfectly - so far.

However, the theory of a comet is totally tossed out of the window when we read the line "When they discovered that the star stopped, they were filled with happiness." A comet is not capable of stopping and staying in the same spot. Therefore, we are given a choice between two possibilities either a star which can move and stop moving, or a comet which could stop moving.

In the end in summation, the Bible states about there was a Star of Bethlehem was a shining object in the sky. It also states it moved to lead those who were Wise Men to the exact location in which Jesus was born and that it then quietly stood over the spot where the little Christ child was sleeping. The Star of Bethlehem quietly fades to the background while the story proceeds to depict the Magi greeting Jesus family and bestowing presents of gold, cinnamon, as well as myrrh.

What is this mysterious object that was associated with the tale that is the Nativity? What did it do to destroy Sodom as well as Gomorrah? What type of craft was visible in the whirlwinds of energy before both Ezekiel as well as Elijah? There are many mysteries unsolved to this day.

Chapter 14: Vimanas From The Vedas

The next installment of supposed experiences with the ancient astronauts we'll turn our attention towards India along with the Vedas. The Vedas are fragments of Hindu text from the ancient civilisations that inhabited in the Indian subcontinent. Over thousands of years,, the Vedas were an oral tradition passed on from one person to another. They weren't completely compiled and recorded until approximately 200 BC. Incredibly, it is believed that the Hindus are of the opinion that Vedas do not have a human origin. the sacred documents are believed to been derived directly from Sky Gods themselves.

There are many Vedas which speak of bizarre flying vehicles known as Vimanas where they claimed that the Sky Gods flew around the skies. The vehicles are typically described as glowing with light, and having the capability of moving "swifter than the mind". The texts convey the impression that the Vimanas can jump from point to point in an instant or with speeds that are faster than the human brain can handle.

The craft appeared to be multi-purpose in nature. They are like modern USOs (unidentified underwater objects) and could submerge in the ocean, as well as glide through the air. The Vimanas were very different in their appearance and design and also. Some were small scout cars but others were massive as tiny cities. These massive ships would arrive and serve as a sort of headquarters or palace in the earth for a few years, before picking them up and taking off to go someplace else.

The Vedas also provide several times regarding the pilots who operated these vessels they were called "Ashvins" which translate roughly to "drivers". They are believed as the "best Charioteers to can reach the skies".

Under the Vimanas were spinning wheels that produced antigravity fields to lift the vehicle and permit it to travel anywhere. Are they the identical "wheels inside wheel" which Ezekiel talked about? They definitely sound similar.

In contrast to Ezekiel's single-time encounter, the early Indians seem to have lived with Vimanas for a number of years and were able to interact with regularly. The Vedas contain numerous stories of Vimanas assisting in last-minute decisions in human affairs, for instance the tale of a man that nearly drowns, only to be saved by the help of a Vimana which appears out of the blue, pulls him from the water, and then carries the man back on dry ground.

In addition, like Ezekiel who compared the work he saw in the form of "living creatures" due to their movement, Indian writers understood the difference between an animal and technological machines. There are passages from the Vedas which describe the intricate details of the Vimanas Propulsion System. Indeed, the full-blown engineering specifications are preserved to be preserved for posterity! Consider this enticing text, for instance:

Durable and sturdy must the structure of the Vimana be constructed, just like an amazing flying bird made of light materials. Inside, one should put in the mercury engine and its heating device made of iron beneath. Through the power contained in the mercury, which causes the whirlwind to drive in motion, the person sitting in the inside can travel a long distance across the sky. The motions that make up the Vimana are so that it can ascend vertically while vertically descending, and then move in a slanting direction, both forwards and backwards. With the aid of these machines, humans can fly through the air, and celestial beings are able to descend to Earth.

The verse makes it evident that the author was aware of what the Vimana could be used for--"with the aid by these devices, humans are able to fly in high-flying air". In addition but he also knew the fact that mercury liquid was utilized for fuel! As modern science suggests that mercury is the ideal fuel for travel in space, it is remarkable. It is possible that what we've got is either an visual account of the event and a basic understanding of a fascinating spacecraft or an incredibly prescient sci-fi writer of the past!

The Vedas clearly distinguish between particular Vimanas which were constructed by humans and operated as well as other Vimanas that were created by the Sky Gods, or in the words of the early astronaut theorists believed ETs, alien visitors. In addition Gods (or ETs) were divided into different factions and often war was fought between the various factions. According to Vedic Scripture, mankind witnessed -- and might have even participated in conflicts that were "fought on land as well as in the air and under the oceans". The Mahabharata states that a god's group also built three massive "cloud fortresses" that sounded similar to space battle stations orbiting in space. From these launch points, they could fight their foes in all directions of the Earth.

Similar conflicts are prevalent in numerous other myths and legends across the globe.

Particularly people have noticed similarities between Hindu stories and the tales of Norse mythology. A lot of the characters and plots in the tales are essentially interchangeable. It is likely not a coincidence as the theory is that in the past, each of Northern European and India were colonized by a small group of people who were referred to by archeologists and historians in the form of "Indo-Europeans".

A clear link that connects Norse mythology as well as Hindu legend is the account of gods fighting one another in battles that arose from thunderbolt-like weapons. As an example Thor, the Norse god Thor is one of the most well-known users of thunderbolts that are weaponized, has an Indian counterpart in the god that is recorded in Sanskrit sources as Tanayitnu.

Thor Of course is known for his amazing weapon Mjolnir. The hammer fires thunderbolts, however it is also a type of "kinetic weapon". Kinetic weapons are tough blunt objects that are hurled at high speed, so that they strike their targets with a tremendous amount of energetic kinetic force. The concept is the same as that of an impact from an asteroid are able to surpass nuclear explosions' power.

It is believed that the US army has been working on these weapons since the beginning during the Vietnam War, when hundreds of tiny projectiles made of metal fell from high elevations in the Vietnamese jungles to inflict death on enemy camps below. The logical follow-up to these experiments in using kinetic energy to create power is known as Project Thor, in which one massive projectile is employed to cause a massive impact on the kinetic field. The project, formally referred to by the name "rods of God" is now attempting to make use of 20-foot long rods dropped from space to completely wipe out entire cities, without the risk that nuclear fallout can bring!

Vimanas? Thor's hammer? What exactly does it mean?

Ancient Astronauts from Egypt and Peru

Egypt is an area of mystery and intrigue. It's a land of mystery and intrigue. North African country can boast one of the oldest civilizations, surpassed perhaps by the ancient Mesopotamia and Egypt is, in fact, has the largest megalithic structures, those ever-elusive monuments to the undiscovered past and the pyramids. The debate about who was responsible for the construction of these massive structures from the early world continues until this day. As the building of such huge structures would be extremely difficult using modern equipment for construction It is almost impossible for an ancient human to achieve such feats. This is what has made ancient astronauts a fantastic space to test their theories about alien visits.

What did the early Egyptians themselves have to say about the subject? Based on Egyptian mythology (or the history of Egypt according to your viewpoint), Egypt was founded in the era of "Zep Tepi" (which literally means "First time") in the year 36,420 BC! If it is true, it will create Egypt older than the ancient Mesopotamia by about thirty thousands of years! According to story, it was at this period in the distant past that gods came out of the sky through their sky-boats and started to construct the megalithic structures we recognize these days as the Pyramids, the sphinx and many other huge structures. They directly ruled over humanity initially before handing over their power to gods who were in essence half-human and half divine.

Ancient Astronaut theorists used these myths in order to make the amazing claim that the first ruling class of Egypt were actually human/alien hybrids! The truth is that rulers from the ancient Egypt are always symbolized in a way with unique appearances. In comparison to the typical human being of the time the rulers of Egypt were slim, with large legs and arms, as well as big heads. The actual size of their heads was typically obscured by the huge Egyptian headdress that was later their crown. Pharaohs.

One of these"hybrid" Egyptian rulers is Akhenaten who has for a long time been called by historians"the "Alien Pharaoh"--if it were only for the purpose of highlight the difference in his style of rule from the standard. Akhenaten was, in addition to having the title of father to Tutankhamen was also known for his efforts to alter the religion that was prevalent in Egypt. Instead of urging his people to adhere to the established theology of polytheistic Egyptian gods Akhenaten did a sudden change of heart and declared that all Egyptians were to worship one god, the sun goddess Aten.

The sudden shift in the way that religion is conducted is similar to the time that the Roman Emperor Constantine the Great was able to make Christianity the law of the country, however it was not to be as effective. A lot of Egyptians began to rebel against the decree of Akhenaten almost immediately. And as shortly as he passed away the priesthood systematically destroyed any monuments or artifacts that were that were associated with him. They also swiftly restored the country to its polytheism of the past.

This was all done under the guidance of Akhenaten's son, and successor the King Tutankhamen. Most people do not know that Tutankhamen's birthname really was "Tutankhaten" which is translated to "the living representation of Aten". Thisnaturally is a question to ask what if King Tut's father believed Tut as a copy copy--a carbon copy of Sun god Aten So, who was Aten and why was it that Tut was created according to his likeness? This very question is a reference to the first chapter of Genesis where God declares, "Let us make man according to our likeness."

Whatever the situation it was a thought that King Tut was apparently trying not to make at any cost. When his father died, Tut changed his name to Tutankhamen. (This is reminiscent of the old joke from history classes of the king of Tut shirking his supposed supremacy by saying "Tutankhaten? Nope! I'm Tutan-Common!

No, I'm not a god! I promise! I'm just a regular man!")

Although Tut may have sought to separate himself from the celestial background that he had inherited Tut was a unique individual with traits that were not common. Similar to his deceased father, Tut had an elongated skull. Research has also proven that this wasn't an isolated anomaly (such as the one caused by the practice of attaching boards to the head of an infant to reduce the size of bones). In fact Tut's skull was more than it was long, and also had greater cranial capacity than the normal human body, which means that it could have more brain capacity.

There isn't much information about the life of King Tut, however, he was a man who lived his life apart from society. He ruled from the time nine years old until the time he died abruptly when he was 18. It is believed that he was murdered by his body, which has the recognizable indications of trauma from blunt force on the skull. But,

Tut was preserved and preserved in the traditional way and was buried with the assurance of a resurrection once gods appeared.

That brings us back to a second significant aspect of the supposed Egyptian connection to ancient astronauts. There is a possibility that the Egyptians could have learned mummification practices either through indirect or direct contact with aliens. Many believe that the practice of mummification was an attempt made by the ancients to emulate an approach used by aliens preserved and maybe even revived their own dead. Others contend that the Egyptians were actually ordered to mummify their dead by extraterrestrials-- and told that when the ETs returned, the mummified corpses would be resurrected.

According to theorles of the ancient astronaut that this is why ancient Egyptians created a sacred burial ritual that was centered around the idea of mummifying their deceased. As we've learned, they didn't just put the bodies of their mummified inside tombs, but they also stuffed them in gold, jewelry and other things that were valuable in the absence of the decedent. This is a sign of their firm conviction that dead people would completely restored when they died "gods" return. It is believed by the Egyptians were so firm in their belief that people who served the deceased ruler would usually let themselves be dead alongside their ruler. They fully believed that once "Reanimation Day" was observed the servants would re-emerge to new life and serve their master again!

The Egyptians weren't the only ancients who practiced mummification. Pre-Columbian people of Peru were very prolific in this method as well. The art of making mummies was practiced in this part that is South America for the better part of 7,000 years. However, the most preserved Mummies date back up to Inca period, which was about 500 years ago.

The Inca often performed rituals of sacrifice to the gods, killing their victims at the tops of mountains, and leaving them in the midst of their gods for them to receive. (Although it is true that the Spanish conquistadors get the blame for their blatant desecration of Native American culture, they deserve some recognition for stopping this ritual of murder that was practiced by both the Inca as well as the Aztecs in North.) However, aside from sacrificial victims the Andean areas of stomping ground of early Peruvian civilization are with Mummies. Similar to the Egyptians as well, the Peruvians were convinced that if they kept the remains of their deceased adequately and preserved them well enough, they would be revived and return to their lives on earth.

The mummies, however, aren't the only thing the ancient people of Peru are famous for. The most famous of them all is those of the Nazca LInes, a series of well-crafted lines that stretch many miles, and creating what some call "runways" in addition to interesting shapes like an enormous monster, spider as well as a mysterious humanoid being. Erich Von Daniken, the famous author of the popular space-based publication Chariots of the Gods, looked over the lines and found that they were more intricate than believed to be, since they contained intricate mathematical equations that were carved into the foothills surrounding.

The lines themselves are relatively new; they were first discovered by people in the 1920s, when pilots saw these lines from the sky. The reason for this is that the most bizarre aspect of these ancient etchings of sand is that it is possible to only be able to see them from the air. Who was it that the airborne attention the Peruvians trying to capture?

The most popular theory is that the elaborate illustrations were just part of a ritual to draw the attention of gods that the Peruvians believed to reside in the heavens. As we've witnessed repeatedly that these gods of the sky and ancient astronauts are interchangeable. Instead of focusing on the person for whom the drawings were created for, we might take a look at the way they were created.

Drawing on the dry Nazca surface is simple. All you need be doing is scratch off the red rock surface and expose the white soil beneath. The fact that rain, powerful winds and other disruptions are extremely uncommon in this region will ensure that the lines that you've created remain in the right place. Therefore, making lines is simple enough and there is no reason to worry about it.

A meaningful illustration that spans miles of barren terrain, in contrast it seems almost impossible unless the artists were aware of the image they created from the in the air. If they could not be able to see it from afar it shouldn't be in a position to comprehend it enough to draw images on earth. This is an obvious question: thousands of years ago, before flight became feasible How were these early Native Americans able to see the whole design from the top up in a way that made an logical sense?

It is possible that they received an assist via a friendly flying object however, a number of other mundane theories have also been suggested in the past. It is likely that Peruvians have developed a hot air balloon in the early days and used it as a way to control massive art works carved through Nazca Plain. Nazca plain. Since there's no evidence similar to this, such theories are merely an unsubstantiated speculation. The real origins and the method of operation that is Nazca Lines remains a mystery. Nazca Lines remains a mystery.

There are some who draw parallels between the enormous panoramas as well as the crops that regularly appear in different parts of the globe. There are certainly some similarities, but beyond the drawings, a major characteristic that is unique to these Nazca Lines is the presence of huge straight lines scattered throughout the landscape. Von Daniken and others contend that these straight lines that run through the desert for miles and are just landing zones for an ancient aircraft from another world.

There is a belief it is possible that Nazca Lines were not just an Native American art project but it was a collective effort of humans and extraterrestrial beings. It was a "learning experience" where ETs in the air above instructed people working below on how to construct the lines. Is this the kind of relationship that the earlier ETs shared with the early Egyptians and even the supposed gold miners from old Mesopotamia? Was it always an example of the ancient astronaut's technological savvy and intelligence aided by the sheer human force?

Ancient Astronauts from
of the Greeks and Romans

The Greco-Roman culture has been recognized as a major ancient civilization not only because of technological advancement, but also for advancements in civic society and philosophy. The Greeks particularly had a head start over their time in a variety of ways. We can owe them for things such as theater and the Olympics and herbal medicines. Historical historians knew that about the fact that the early Greeks were an intelligent bunch however, in 1900 when researchers discovered an ancient Greek shipwreck on the coast of Antikythera, a Mediterranean island known as Antikythera all we believed we were aware of Greek knowledge was removed from the equation.

At the bottom of the long-submerged vessel was a obscure cargo from antiquity. Alongside statues and everyday artifacts, it was an odd piece of machinery made up of intricate cogwheels, gears and other moving components and enclosed in a gold-and-wood case. What was this thing? What purpose did it serve? And who designed it? It certainly was beyond any technology that was known to the antiquated Greeks.

A closer investigation revealed that the item was a type of analog computer. The device was an automated computer that was just a few thousand years before its time, being built before the time that the abacus even invented. It also appeared to have features that could have let the user observe the cycle of the moon, sun as well as other planetary and celestial objects. They were also not just estimates; the exacting accuracy of this device would never be replicated until at the very least the 19th century.

If anything it stands out as modern Greek technology. However, ancient theories of astronauts suggest that it's more than a simple prototype. They believe that aliens either instructed humans to create the device, or they created it by themselves and gave the device to humans as an offering.

The Greeks have indeed claimed an extensive history of celestial visitors who came from the heavens to give gifts. Think about the myth of Prometheus in the early days of Greek mythology. Prometheus was a part of a primordial group of beings known as the Titans who traveled to Earth in the distant past. The Titans had a version in The Starfleet's "Prime Directive" and were prohibited from directly interfering in the affairs of humanity.

Prometheus however, decided to take to heart the plight of the poor of humanity and overturned the rule of non-interference by educating primitive people how to build and make use of fire. It could seem like a benign enough gesture to teach the caveman how to light an open flame in his cave to warm it up, however this tiny gesture of goodwill was sufficient to earn the respect of all Prometheus' celestial friends. It was Zeus, the Greek god Zeus who slayed the hammer after shackling the fugitive Titan to a mountaintop, in which an eagle was to be able to spend the rest of its life gnawing in his liver.

This will teach him, won't it? What does all this mean? Do you think there is more to this story than what is apparent? Could it be possible that the whole Greek Pantheon of gods and goddesses was actually an ancient spaceship? If yes, what was the reason why some decided to leave the group and risk everything to aid humanity? What side are we really on? Or are we just players caught between two sides? Maybe there were always two rival factions of ancient astronauts fighting to be the best.

The renowned Roman historian from the Jewish world Josephus could have witnessed this epic battle in the year 65 AD , when he was in attendance for what sounded much like a massive UFO sighting above Israel. The event was described by Josephus in the following manner: "On the 21st of the month of Artemisium it was reported that there was the appearance of a supernatural phenomenon, which was later disproved by faith. In fact, what I'm about to discuss could, as I believe, be considered as a fairy tale, if not for the story of eyewitnesses, and the subsequent catastrophes that deserved to be acknowledged. Since, before sunset in all of the nation the sight of chariots was seen flying through the air, and armoured battalions soaring through the clouds and over city after city." Be aware that what Josephus and others witnessed as they traveled across the sky was so unbelievable the fact that Josephus acknowledges that he couldn't believe it if didn't have seen it! It is clear from this quote how amazing the event was.

There is a Roman historical writer Plutarch also reported an amazing UFO sighting. This happened in the year the year 74 BC and involved a large number of soldiers moving through Turkey to destroy Mithridates VI's army. Mithridates VI. As per Plutarch, "With no apparent changes in the weather, but all of a sudden the sky was ripped apart and a massive flame-like body was seen to fall in between both armies. Its form was similar to a wine jar, and in its color, resembled melting silver. The marvel, it is said, took place in Phrygia located in the area known as Otries." The two armies of the world were set to battle when a massive UFO fell down between the two. What do we think of these cosmic interruptions? What message are these vessels and their crew members trying to send?

If you were to question Constantine the Great who was the Roman Emperor who brought in the period of Roman Catholic Christianity, the message was fairly obvious. Before Constantine was the emperor, he was leading an army of soldiers fighting at the Milvian Bridge near Rome when the bridge was suddenly illuminated and a cross flying in the skies! When he saw this UFO in cruciform, Constantine heard the words "by this sign, you will overcome" in his head.

Constantine was clearly stunned by the incident and was unsure of what to think of it initially. However, the next night the vision he received revealed everything in a clear way. According to Constantine his story, he was visited by no other than Jesus Christ, who told him to put the symbol that represented the Cross on the standard of his troops. According to the legend, Constantine did indeed conquer following this and brought the broken Roman Empire back together , and ultimately becoming Emperor himself.

Through the years, many have suggested that Constantine's vision could have been altered after the fact or simply made up as a ploy to further Constantine's goals. However, Constantine himself did not alter his story and always claimed that what he witnessed was a fact. He was believed to believe the story and the question could be the interpretation he made of what he witnessed.

The third century AD when Constantine observed this object in the third century AD, the whole world was filled with spiritual mysticism. If something strange happened it was immediately contemplated in terms of the spiritual. A few people consider the possibility that an object flying through the air could be a technology. In the present we have aircrafts that we own, and even primitive spacecraft. If we could see an odd cigar- or cross-shaped thing floating in the sky, we'd be less likely to attribute a supernatural quality to it.

However, if it wasn't God but rather ancient astronauts who revealed their presence to

Constantine What did they want to accomplish? (And they clearly were seeking to achieve something; simply seeing objects in the skies may be an accident however, being able to hear a voice and experiencing an image of Christ are a different story altogether!) You can believe what you want however, there are a few conspiracy theorists who believe ETs have been trying to influence world events using religion.

If this was the scenario, it makes perfect sense to focus on Constantine who was a rising general already on track to take over the Roman Empire. When Constantine was in charge his position, he could be able to enforce his dictates to the people and make an empire that had once served Christians to lions a haven for Christ in a matter of hours. Naturally, God His own word could've predicted the event as easily as any of the ancient astronaut or the people that prefer Christianity to conspiracy theories believe that the events in Milvian Bridge was just as Constantine saw it as a divine action to convert to Christianity the Roman Empire.

Like everything else, it depends on how you interpret the events.

Chapter 15: Conclusion Thoughts

Many believe that Earth is visited by aliens as well as spacecraft is this really feasible? Stories of unidentified flying objects have been trickling through the years echoing events from the past. In the 1940's, the term "flying saucer" was a regular part of the language of an enthralled world. It was as if the skies were brimming with UFO's of every kind. Through the years UFO's were seen by every level of society. even astronauts witnessed UFO's.

"I myself believe strongly in UFOs and I was a believer in UFO's long before I got involved in Space Programs. I believe the existence of other cultures out there, that we are traveling from.

It was the early 1950's, when I was piloting fighters from Germany and these aircraft were passing over our base, and looked like the types of formations we use with our jet fighters. Sometimes their movements were more unpredictable than ours. This meant that they were able to move in real time;

speed up laterally, accelerate forward and aft faster than we could. We found them to look similar to fighters flying high however they did not have wings.

They certainly were higher and faster than the planes that we've seen today on Earth at that time. They certainly seemed to be saucer-shaped and made of metal."

- Colonel Gordon Cooper

Why are UFOs so hidden and mysterious? If aliens are visiting Earth there are some who think this question should be resolved only through directly speaking with UFOs. In 1977, NASA put two of its robotic Voyager spacecraft on exploration mission towards Jupiter, Saturn, Uranus and Neptune which are the four largest outer planets. The epic voyage took 12 years to complete , yet they collected more scientific information on our solar system than has been uncovered in the previous 500 years. Maybe this is what the UFO's mission is to the planet Earth and to study our planet for an advanced technology-driven civilization in the far space.

We are aware that the chances of locating intelligent life within our solar system are very unlikely. Our sun is only one of many billions of stars in our galaxy. The Milky Way Galaxy, our galaxy, is just one of the billions of galaxies that are scattered across the universe. In the face of these odds, do we really believe we are the only ones on this planet? In the month of August, 1996, scientists revealed that life may have was present on Mars. In the previous months the first known planet orbiting another sun was found to be eight light years away which is a staggering 50 trillion miles away from Earth on a cosmic scale which is literally away from our backyard. Nowadays, we have a lot of knowledge about the universe, and it is possible that there is life on the other side, however, the majority of what you read about it is just nonsense. The reason is that people are willing to believe the most absurd stories with no evidence and there are numerous stories from around the globe of people who have seen odd light sources on the Earth. Many of these tales are actually true and there are lights that appear strange in the sky, however they are usually explained.

There are all sorts of strange things happening all around us, and most people don't be aware of this, and so they notice something strange and think, "Wow, that must be from an extraterrestrial world." This is why there is a lot of trust in the globe.

I believe that the strongest evidence points to UFO's having an extra-terrestrial origin. However, UFO's have been around Earth since the beginning of time. These UFO's from Earth are often traveling to a space under the oceans. It could be that some UFO's were commanded by angels, and piloted by gray aliens.

www.ingramcontent.com/pod-product-compliance
Lightning Source LLC
Chambersburg PA
CBHW060326030426
42336CB00011B/1214